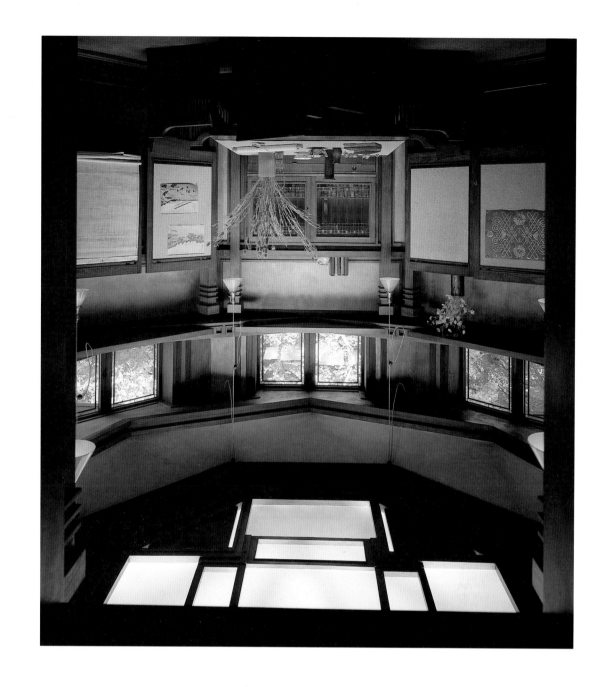

Oak Park

The Genius of Frank Lloyd Wright

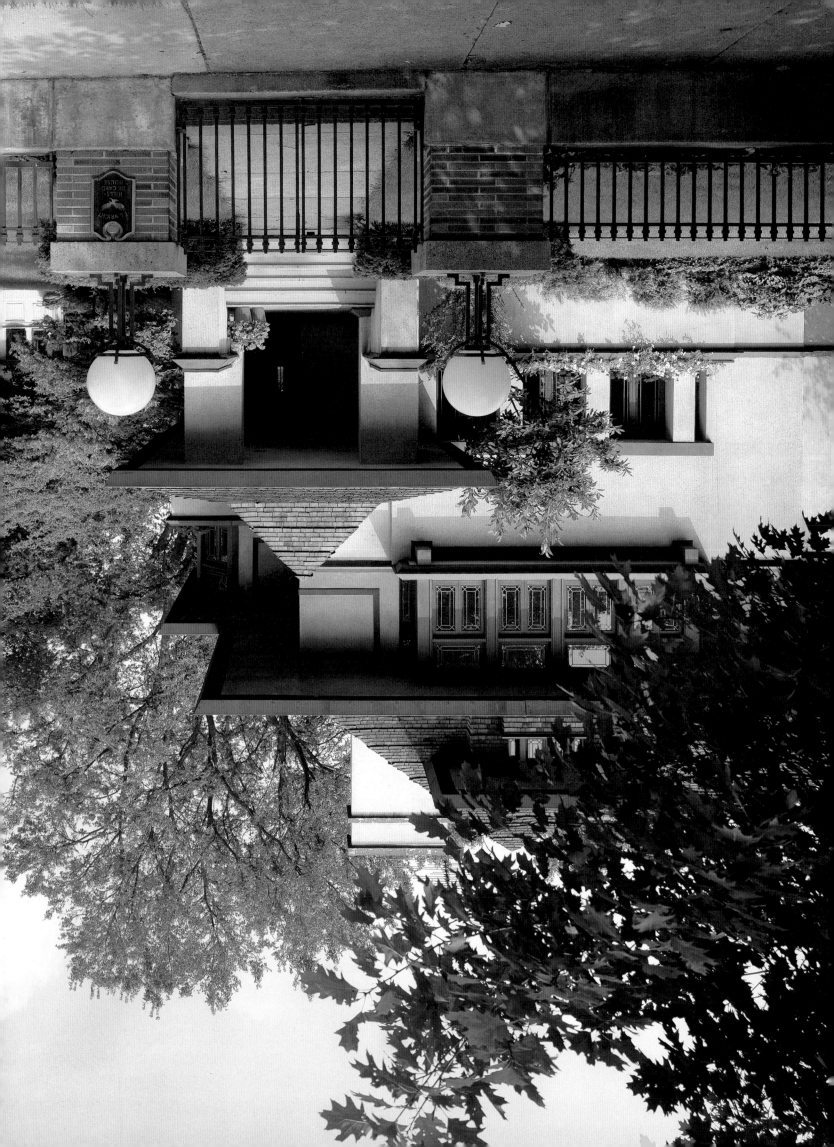

The Genius of Frank Lloyd Wright

Oak Park

Robin Langley Sommer
Photography by Balthazar and Christian Korab

BARNES
&NOBLE
BOOKS
NEW YORK

This Edition published by
Barnes & Noble Inc.
by arrangement with Brompton Books
Corporation

Produced by Brompton Books Corporation
15 Sherwood Place
Greenwich, CT 06830

ISBN 0-7607-0062-1

Printed in China

Reprinted 1998, 2001

All pictures courtesy Balthazar and Christian Korab except
where noted:
Courtesy of The Art Institute of Chicago: page 11 (top)
Brompton Picture Library: page 19
Buffalo and Erie County Historical Society: page 20
(bottom right)
© **Dennis McClunden:** page 7
© **The Frank Lloyd Wright Foundation:** pages 13, 18
**Frank Lloyd Wright Home and Studio Foundation,
Oak Park, IL:** pages 6, 10

Page 1: The library at the Frank Lloyd Wright Home and Studio.
The octagonal shape of the library is repeated in the shelves,
ceiling trim and skylights.

Page 2: In recognition of the DeCaro's restoration of the E.R.
Hills House, the Oak Park Landmarks Commission renamed this
home the E.R. Hills-DeCaro House.

Page 5: Wright's masterpiece in poured concrete, Unity Temple,
has been designated by the American Institute of Architects as
one of 17 American buildings designed by Wright to be
preserved as examples of his contribution to architecture.

Contents

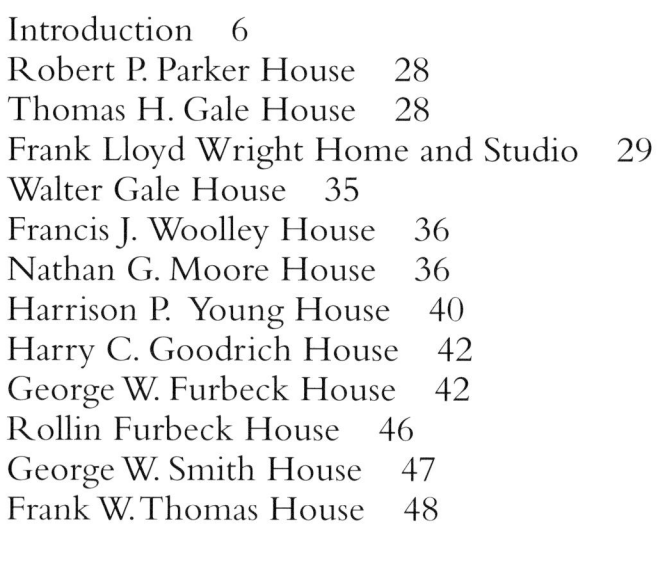

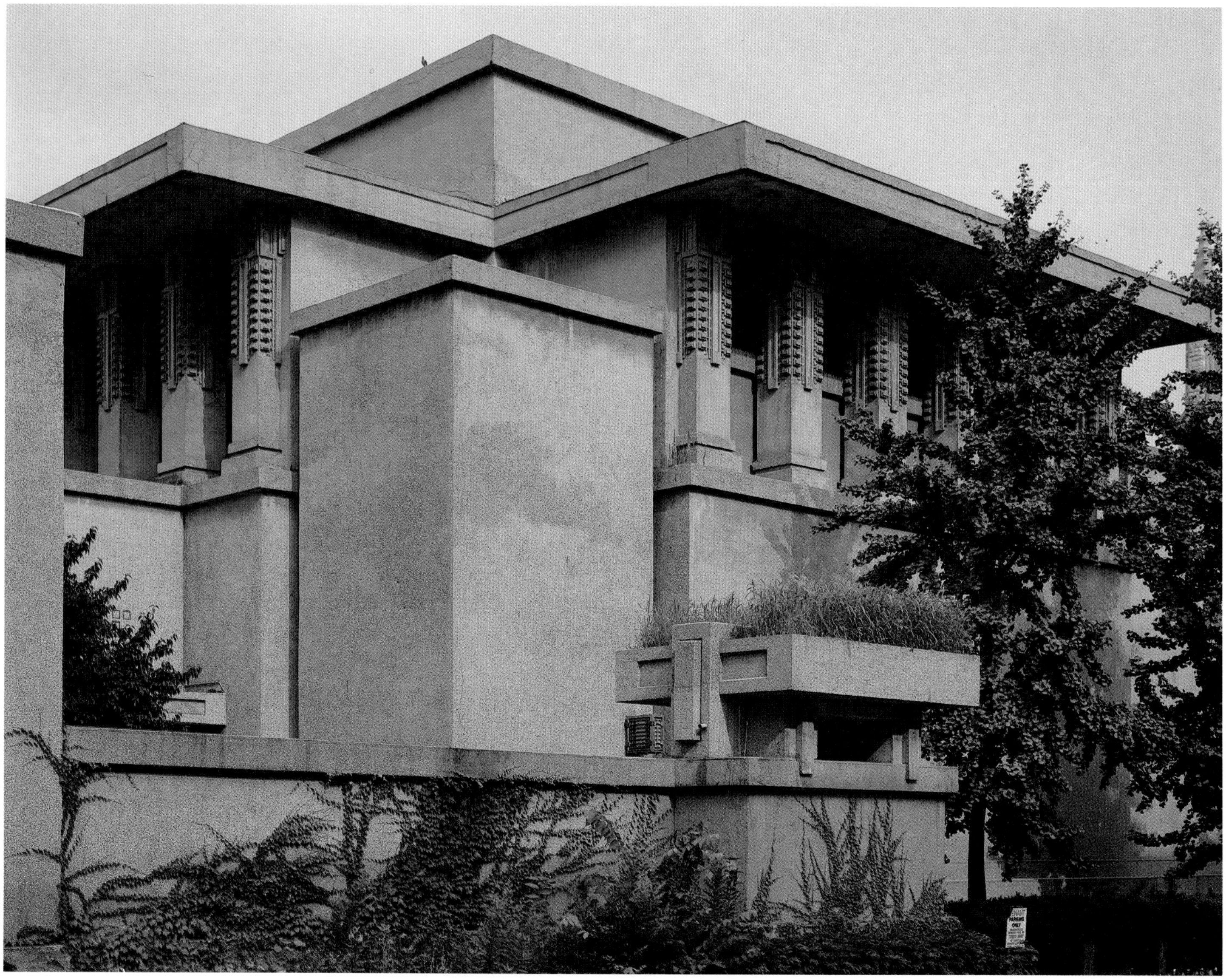

Introduction

The Chicago suburb of Oak Park, which still looks much as it did a hundred years ago, was a uniquely suitable environment for a young man of Frank Lloyd Wright's background and ambitions. His father, William Cary Wright, was a native New Englander (he left the family in 1885, when Wright was eighteen years old), and his mother, Anna Lloyd Jones, came from a prosperous farming family of Welsh origin in Spring Green, Wisconsin. Their only son was born in Richland Center, Wisconsin, in 1867. Both families had strong commitments to education and the ministry, combining elements of New England Transcendentalism with the Lloyd Jones' Unitarian heritage.

When Wright moved to Oak Park at the age of twenty-one, he had already spent several years studying architecture and civil engineering at the University of Wisconsin, although he never took his degree. Since 1887, he had been employed as a draftsman by Louis Sullivan and his partner, Dankmar Adler, in their thriving Chicago office. When Wright became engaged to Catherine Tobin, Sullivan advanced him the money to buy a lot and build in Oak Park, where he had been living with his mother and sisters. The community was securely established and prosperous, settled mainly by transplanted Congregationalists from New England. Church services, lectures, and concerts were the principal pastimes (the town had no saloons, which earned it the nickname "Saints' Rest" in boisterous Chicago). Its broad, tree-lined streets were studded with houses in the fashionable styles of the day: Queen Anne, Victorian, Gothic, and neo-Colonial.

Always anticlassical in his attitude toward architecture, Wright was vehement in his criticism of these derivative styles (although he found it expedient to conform to them in some early Oak Park commissions "bootlegged" during his six-year tenure with Adler & Sullivan). In his book *Drawings and Plans of Frank Lloyd Wright: The Early Period (1893-1909)*, the young architect took aim at American styles: "The ideals of Ruskin and Morris and the teaching of the Beaux Arts have hitherto prevailed in America, steadily confusing, as well as in some respects revealing to us our opportunities. . . . Our better-class residences are chiefly tributes to English architecture, cut open inside and embellished to suit; porches and 'conveniences' added: the result in most cases a pitiful mongrel."

Wright's deep admiration for the innovative work of Louis Sullivan, despite the rift that developed between them in 1893, was a major influence. But he took Sullivan's credo "form follows function" one step further. In Wright's view, form and function were one. The house and studio that he built at 351 Chicago Avenue between 1889 and 1897 became a microcosm of his early work and a precursor of many projects then far in the future. The original house was a simple, six-room cube with a high triangular gable and casement windows, clad in cedar shingles. The design was sniffed at as "seaside" by some Oak Park neighbors, and it was certainly influenced by the cottages being built by Bruce Price and other Eastern architects. It also recalls the shingle-style work of Joseph Lyman Silsbee, for whom Wright had worked briefly as a draftsman and

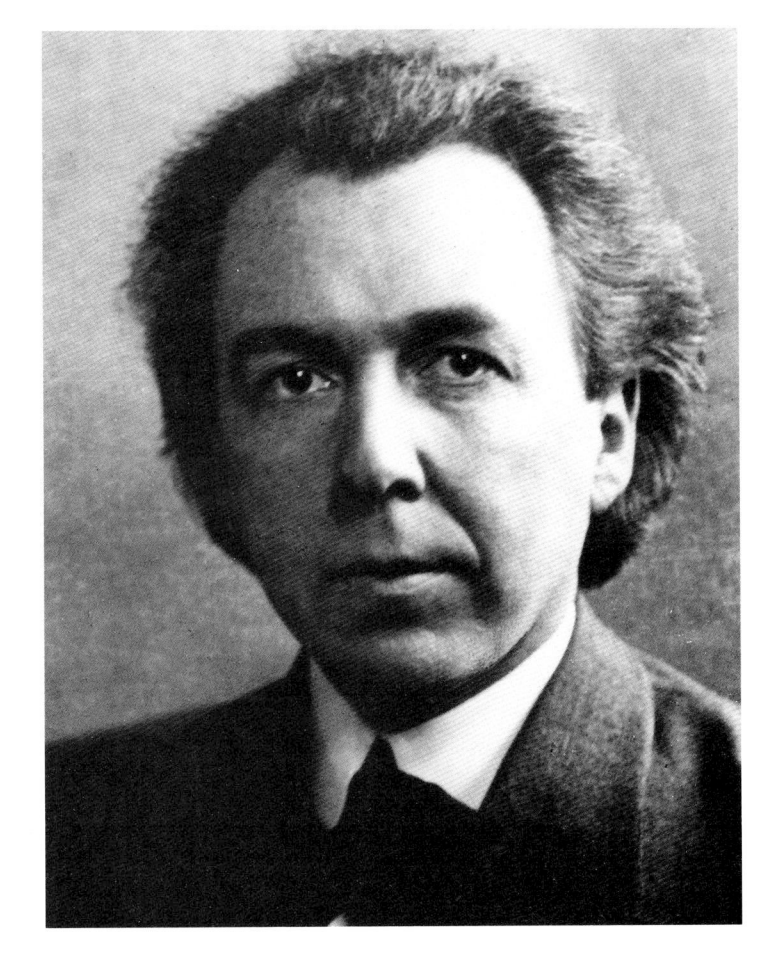

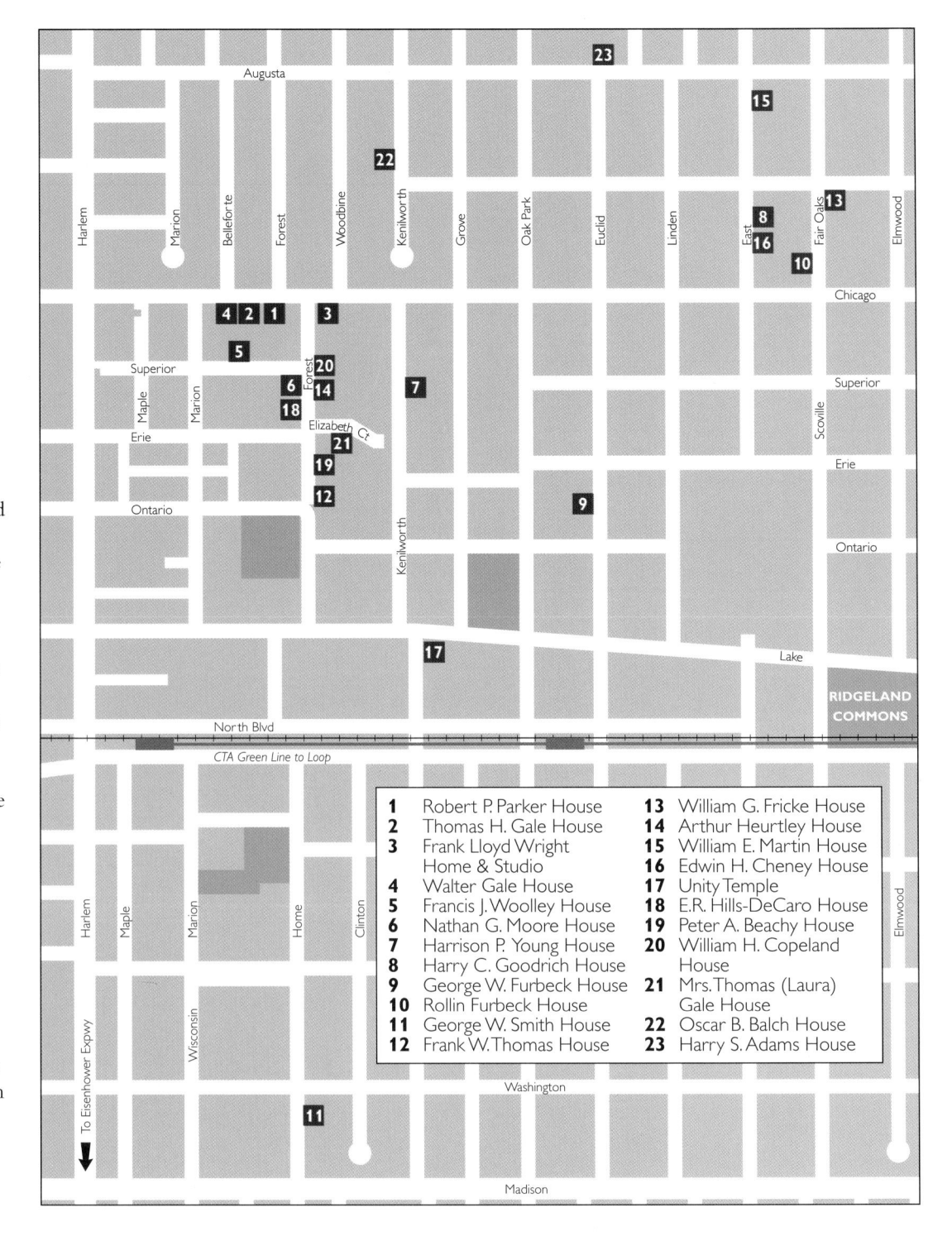

Opposite bottom: Frank Lloyd Wright ten years after he left Adler & Sullivan to practice architecture on his own. He was small in stature, but he had a commanding presence that made him seem larger than life to his associates.

Right: A map of Oak Park, including the landmark houses designed by Wright, many of them clustered in the quadrant formed by North Kenilworth, Chicago, and Forest Avenues, and Lake Street. Unity Temple is at Lake Street and Kenilworth, opposite the Post Office, and the Wright Home and Studio at Chicago and Forest Avenues.

Following pages: The Frank Lloyd Wright Home and Studio, with the octagonal library at right. The handsome complex grew like Topsy from the original residence of 1889 to accommodate the needs of Wright's growing family and successful practice.

1	Robert P. Parker House	**13**	William G. Fricke House
2	Thomas H. Gale House	**14**	Arthur Heurtley House
3	Frank Lloyd Wright Home & Studio	**15**	William E. Martin House
		16	Edwin H. Cheney House
4	Walter Gale House	**17**	Unity Temple
5	Francis J. Woolley House	**18**	E.R. Hills-DeCaro House
6	Nathan G. Moore House	**19**	Peter A. Beachy House
7	Harrison P. Young House	**20**	William H. Copeland House
8	Harry C. Goodrich House		
9	George W. Furbeck House	**21**	Mrs. Thomas (Laura) Gale House
10	Rollin Furbeck House		
11	George W. Smith House	**22**	Oscar B. Balch House
12	Frank W. Thomas House	**23**	Harry S. Adams House

who had designed the Unitarian Church of All Souls for Wright's uncle, minister Jenkin Lloyd Jones.

The first-floor plan comprised an entry into a small hallway that gave onto the living room, whose chief feature was a fireplace in an inglenook, its surround of Roman pressed brick. The fireplace would hold a preeminent place in Wright's residential designs throughout his career, appearing in many forms and materials as "the heart of the house." The dining room and kitchen, at the rear of the house, gave onto a long, narrow back porch. Upstairs was a studio, the master bedroom, a bath, and a nursery for the first of the Wrights' six children, Frank Lloyd Wright, Junior (called Lloyd).

As the family grew, so did the house. In 1895 Wright extended it east from the kitchen to make a servant's room and a new kitchen, with a striking barrel-vaulted playroom above, complete with fireplace, art-glass windows, built-in seating and lighting fixtures, and a handsome mural. Stringcourses (horizontal bands or moldings) defined doorways, windows, and other spatial elements in new ways that would become a design signature. The dining room became a study when a new bay was added to the original kitchen to create a dining area on the sunlit side of the house. The octagon was introduced in a bay added to the north wall of the living room and became a prominent feature in

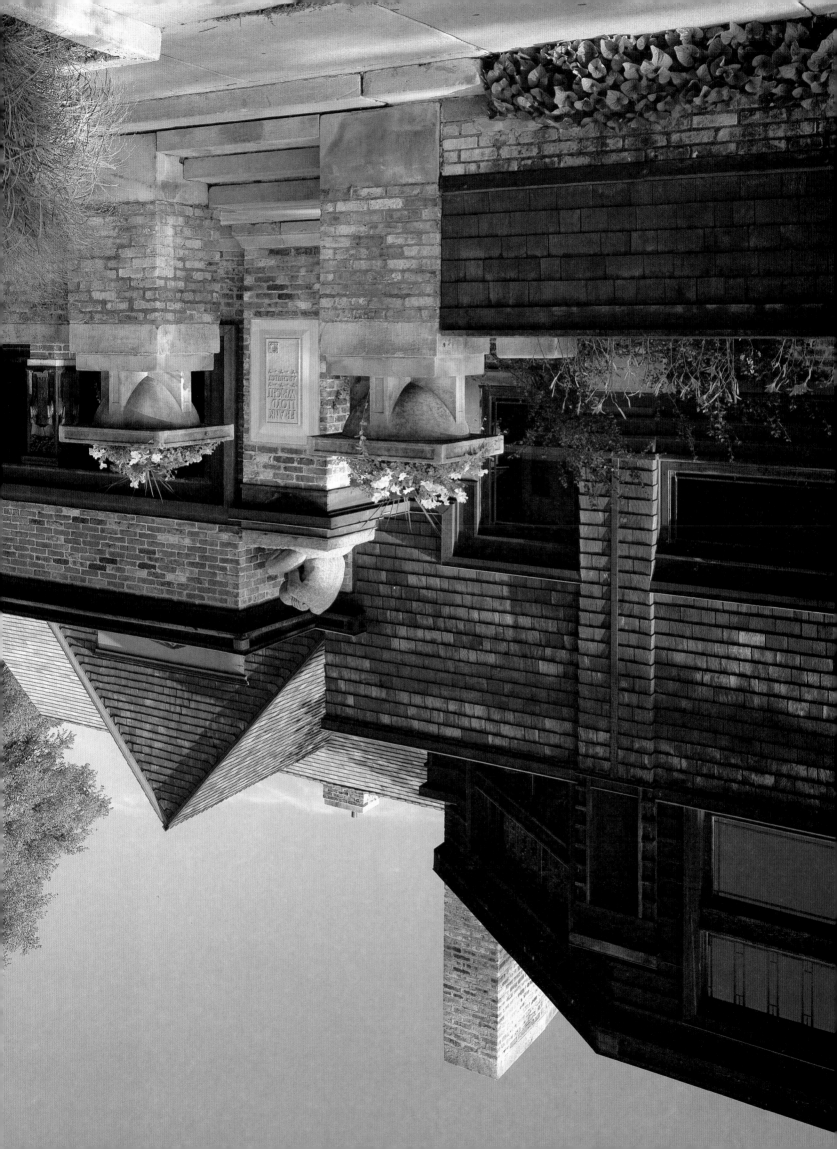

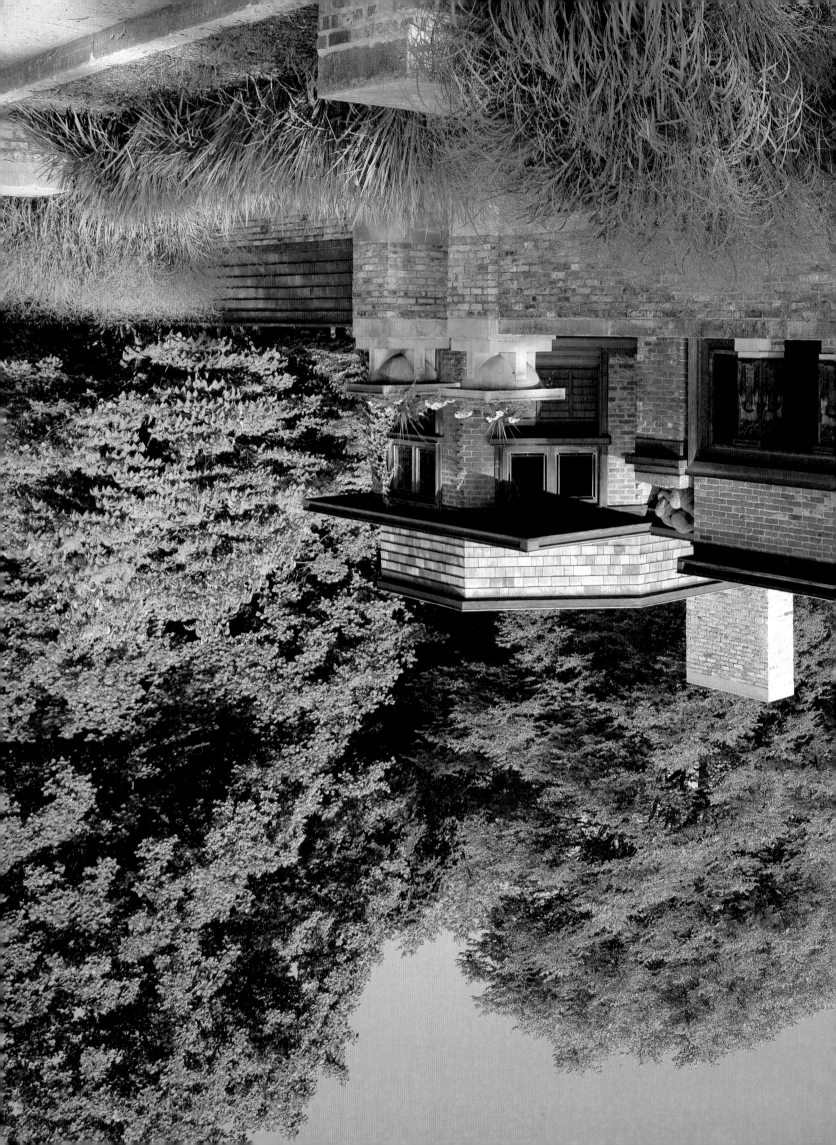

room to Frank Lloyd Wright was space, not the walls surrounding the space, but 'the space within to be lived in,' as Wright quoted Lao Tse."

At his home studio, a band of young assistants and office manager Isabel Roberts helped Wright carry out the commissions that came in growing numbers, including many from friends and admirers in Oak Park, where he had designed his first house in 1892 – actually two houses, built on Chicago Avenue for Thomas H. Gale. They are intimately related in design, both being in the Queen Anne style with rectilinear innovations that show Wright's movement toward his own Prairie style. It is believed, according to Storrer, that Thomas Gale built what would be the Robert P. Parker house, at 1019 Chicago Avenue, as an investment, in partnership with his brother, Walter Gale. His own dwelling was at 1027 Chicago Avenue and Walter's at 1031.

Both the Thomas H. Gale house and the Parker residence have two-story octagonal bays, differing slightly in the treatment of the second-story windows. The main floor of each includes a traditional front entry

subsequent additions – a means of breaking down the square. On the second floor, the original studio was divided by a low wall, or screen, in the Japanese mode, to provide separate quarters for the girls and boys.

More radical innovations appeared in the design for a separate studio, adjacent to the house and connected to the study by a passageway (1897). Its complex double entrance and hall, octagonal library, and two-story drafting room lighted by clerestory windows, with a balcony suspended in part by heavy iron chains, became a showpiece for his clients (although he also maintained a Chicago office, in the Rookery Building, during this period). From 1906, the entrance to the studio was off Chicago Avenue by way of a terrace that led to a narrow covered portico flanked by sculptures by Richard Bock, a gifted collaborator who worked with Wright on many projects. The compression of space in and around the entry heightened the sense of expectation about the building's interior. As Wright historian William Allin Storrer explains in *The Frank Lloyd Wright Companion* (University of Chicago Press, 1993), ''A

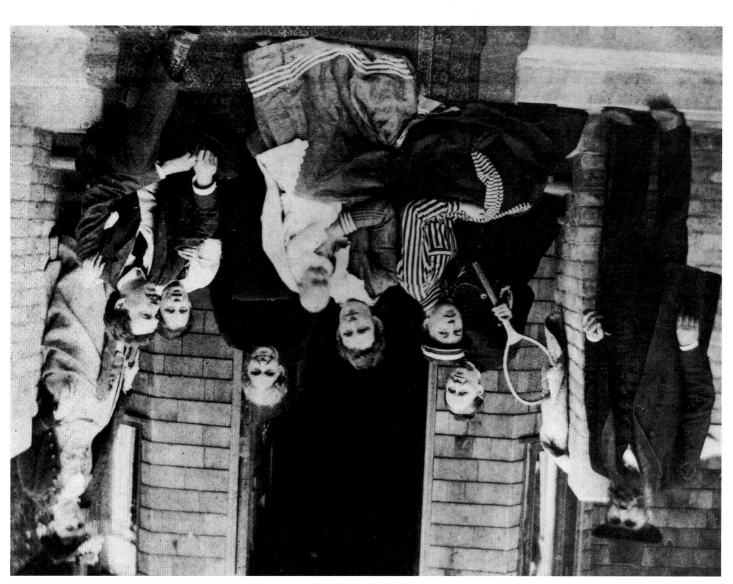

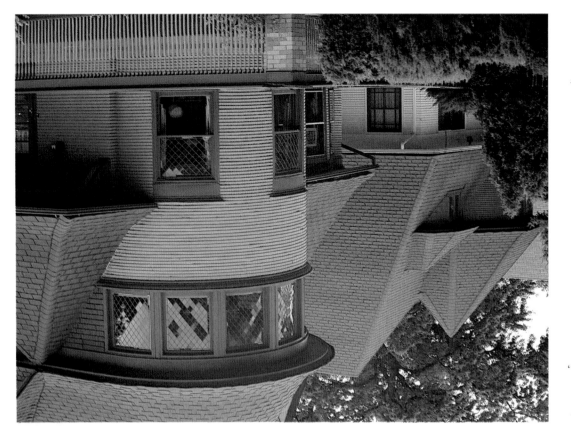

Opposite top: Wright, seated on steps, at home in Oak Park with, from left, his uncle, Jenkin Lloyd Jones, aunt Susan, sister Jane, wife Catherine holding their first child, Lloyd, mother Anna Lloyd Wright, sister Maginel, and cousin Mary.

Top right: Architect Dankmar Adler, Louis Sullivan's partner in the influential Chicago firm that built the nation's first modern skyscraper. Wright worked for Adler & Sullivan for six years and was deeply influenced by the experience.

Right: The Thomas H. Gale and Walter Gale houses, in the Queen Anne style, side by side on West Chicago Avenue.

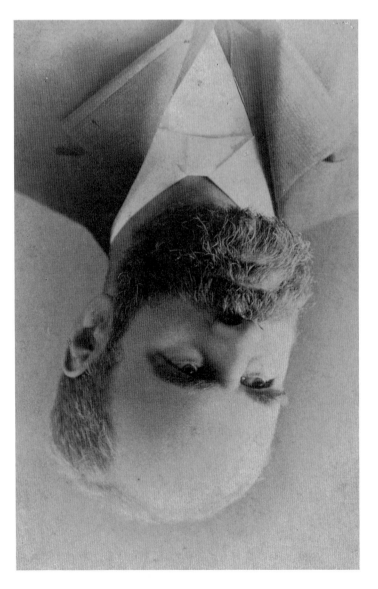

Flanked by a reception room. The centrally placed library (living room) opens onto a porch and into the dining room, adjacent to the kitchen and a second, smaller, porch. The rooflines are steeply pitched, and the roofs have relatively wide overhangs where they meet the second-story windows and the entry porches. A porch intended for the side of the Parker house was never built, and the existing front porch has a post-and-lintel construction rather than the half-octagon without supports originally planned by Wright.

Immediately west of the Thomas H. Gale house is the house built for his brother Walter Gale in 1893, shortly after Wright left Adler & Sullivan to open his own office. A handsome building in the Queen Anne style, the house has many attractive features, including a spacious entry hall with beaded-edge wood paneling. To the left is a large self-contained reception room. Straight ahead is the library (living room) and the dining room, both with tiled fireplaces. A short passage leads to the kitchen, pantry, and stairs.

At the stairwell landing, an octagonal bay with seating provides good lighting. Upstairs, curved diamond-paned windows culminate in a casement window at each end – a feature that would become increasingly important in Wright's fenestration. The three-story turret suggests the influence of Silsbee, who was a master of the Queen Anne style, with its rounded towers, pillared front piazzas, and large bay windows. A narrow

from England and modified to American needs, is apparent in the woodwork, tiled fireplaces, and many other interior details. Wright was a close friend of Englishman C. R. Ashbee, a force in disseminating Arts and Crafts ideals.

Another commission of 1893 was the house designed for Francis and Cora L. Woolley at 1030 Superior Street. This conventional design, back-to-back with the Parker House on Chicago Avenue, was originally covered with clapboard siding to the second-floor sill line and clad with shingles to the soffit (roof overhang). Regrettably, it has been covered with vinyl siding in recent years. The entry porch, facing the street, is reached by a

dormer rising two stories provides a counterpoint to the building's rounded forms. The second-floor plan includes two large bedrooms, a dressing room and bath, a servant's room, and ample closets with built-in drawers and linen shelves. The third floor housed servants' quarters, including a bath, at a time when live-in domestic help was still a commonplace in well-off middle-class households.

The original front terrace was restored in 1977 and extensive restoration was done in the 1980s. Of the three houses built for the Gale brothers on this block of Chicago Avenue, the Walter Gale residence is widely considered the most attractive and interesting. The influence of the popular Arts and Crafts style, imported

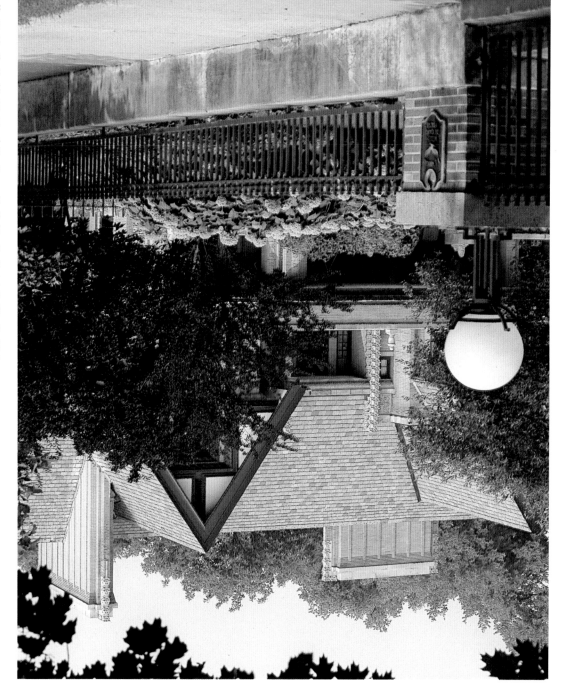

Left: The Nathan G. Moore house, as rebuilt to Wright's design after the 1922 fire that gutted the original structure, commissioned by Moore in 1894. Wright's modifications to the Tudor style his client requested included a capacious porch and massive horizontal chimneys crowning the slate roof.

Opposite bottom: Wright's 1893 drawing for the William H. Winslow house in River Forest, a forerunner of the Prairie house. Its stylobate foundation and horizontal lines united house and site in a new way that created both admiration and controversy in nearby Oak Park. The frieze at the second level shows Sullivan's influence.

flight of steps with a low wall on either side. Originally, the first floor included a reception room flanked by a parlor that opened to the library. Both these living areas have shallow bays extending to the second floor. The dining room and kitchen, with pantry, at the back of the house, had the customary rear entry for servants and tradesmen. The upstairs bedrooms were arranged around the hall along Wright's usual lines, which provided for three kinds of residential space: traffic areas, including entries and hallways; principal activities space, including living room or library; and ancillary services space, including dining room, kitchen, bedrooms, and baths. Outside, extension of the lower-floor exterior to the second-floor sill line is comparable to the treatment of the Rollin Furbeck house and other designs of this period.

Nathan G. Moore, an attorney, was living across the street from the Wrights in 1894, when the young architect became the talk of Oak Park for the innovative house he had designed for William H. Winslow in nearby River Forest. The Moores admired Wright, but they wanted a traditional house – an English Tudor with full half-timbering. In fact, they brought photographs of Tudor houses to their meeting with Wright.

Moore retained him with the proviso that "We don't want you giving us anything like that house you did for Winslow. I don't fancy sneaking down back streets to my morning train just to avoid being laughed at" (*Autobiography*, p. 128).

Against his inclinations, Wright designed an attractive and livable mansion in the Tudor style, which was becoming extremely popular. He was soon swamped with requests for similar designs. To his chagrin, the Moore house was considered just as successful as the Winslow house. However, he always rejoiced in the fact that he had introduced an authentic American porch, unique to any Tudor house on British or American soil.

The original Moore house was a cross-gabled structure of Roman brick with a steeply pitched tile roof. The porch faced south, and entry was from the northern side. The centrally located entrance hall was floored with oak and faced the stairwell. The first-floor rooms were on a grand scale: a large living room with bay window, library, reception room, dining room, and a conservatory, as well as the kitchen and butler's pantry. The small wing to the west was intended as a garden house but remained unfurnished. Upstairs, there were six bed-

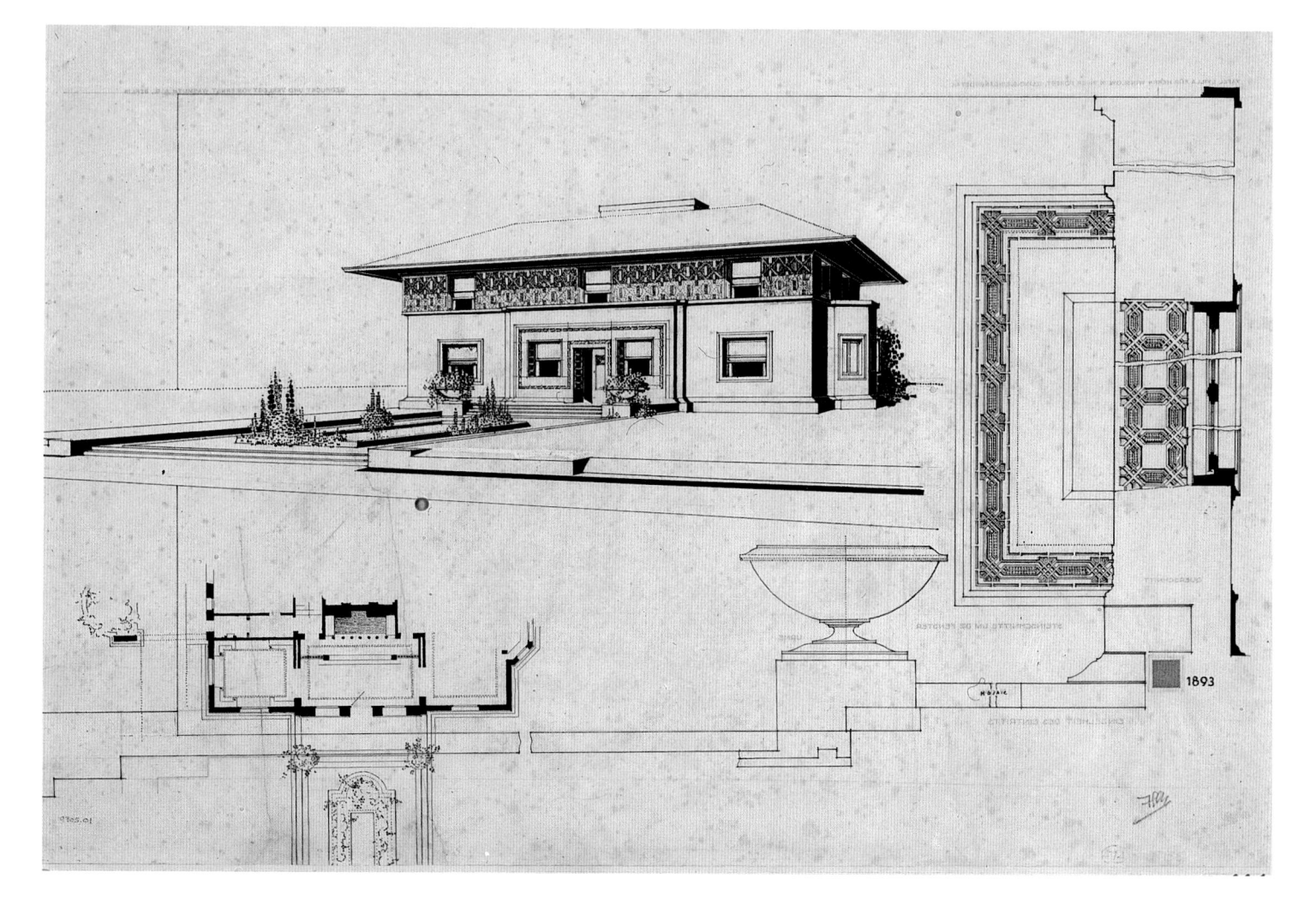

rooms – the two in front shared a balcony – a bath, and numerous closets.

The house was gutted by fire in 1922, and the Moores retained Wright for the remodeling. The structure was entirely rebuilt above the first floor; in some places, from the foundations. At this time, the roof was extended downward, from just above the second-floor window lintels to the first-floor lintel line. Chimneys were enlarged, the former tile roof replaced by slate, and the horizontal trim removed. The result, with the addition of several Japanese touches, was a house even more imposing than the original.

The 1895 commission for the Harrison P. Young house involved remodeling and adding to an existing house at 334 North Kenilworth Avenue. Wright's plan called for moving the wide-clapboard structure back 16½ feet in order to add a new living room, a wide porch, and two second-floor bedrooms to the front of the house.

The north end of the narrow-clapboard porch, built on the original foundations, cantilevers over the driveway, and the new living room, which runs the width of the house, has windows onto the porch to increase interior light. An octagonal bay brings additional light into the reception room, which is screened from the hallway by Tuscan columns and spindles – this use of

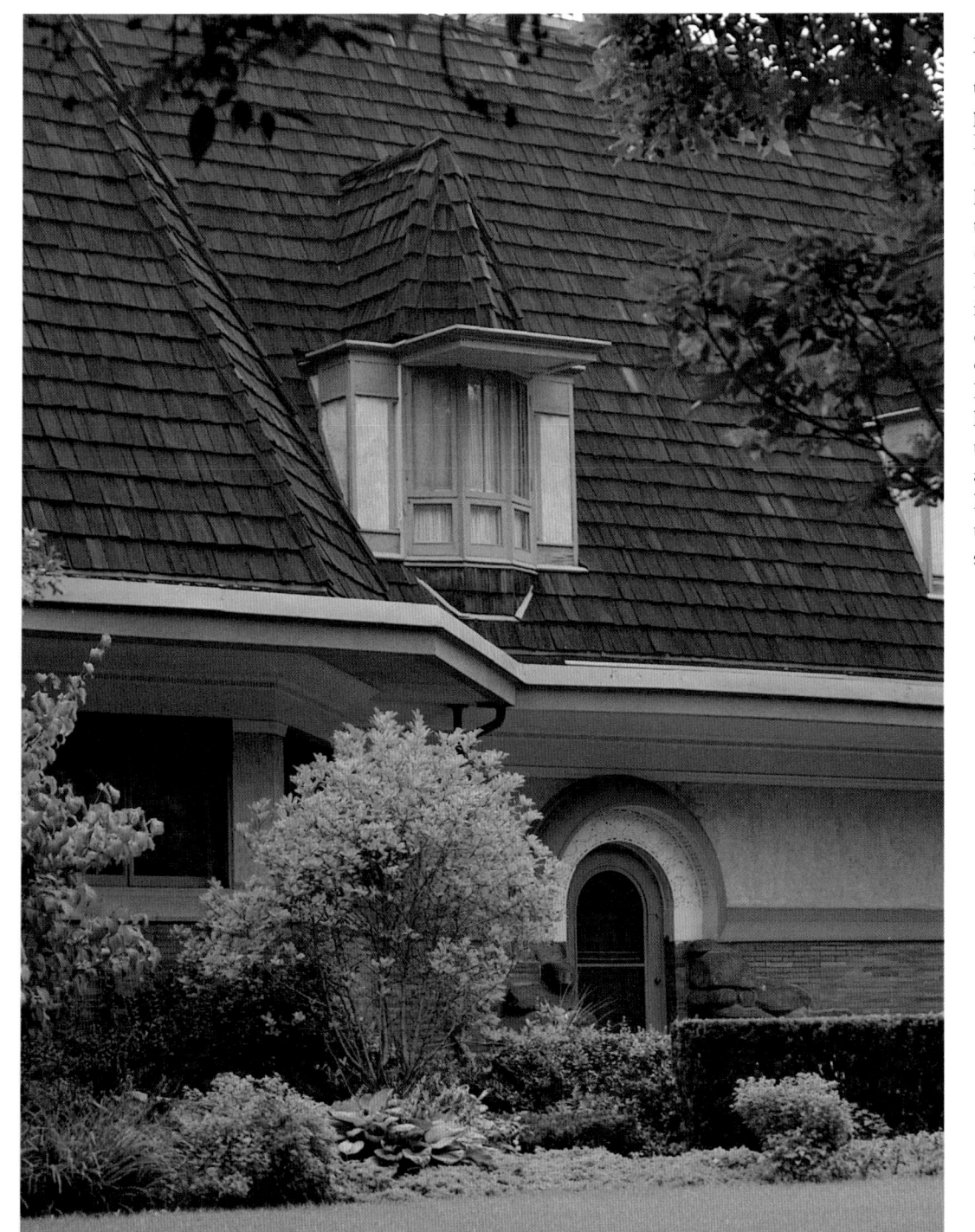

Left and opposite: One of Wright's earliest design signatures was the indirect, compressed entryway under a Roman arch, as seen in the 1895 Chauncey L. Williams house in River Forest (left) and the Arthur Heurtley residence (1902) in Oak Park. The use of Roman brick for both exteriors is carried out in the arched entrys, approached indirectly to create a sense of shelter and heighten expectancy about the living space within. The evolution toward the Prairie style is apparent in the later Heurtley house, with its strong horizontal thrust and brick coursework suggestive of board and batten.

screening is a feature that recurs in almost all the designs of the period.

There is a Wright fireplace in both living room and master bedroom with handsome beaded work in the mantels, which rise in widening tiers from base to top. The fireplace surround is of glazed brick set in narrow Roman courses, with rounded corners. Wright's meticulous hand is also seen in the red brass hardware throughout the house and in the egg-and-dart detailing in the den.

The entry steps have been restored. They parallel the porch, leading toward the cantilevered end. The south end of the porch has been enclosed, and imitation half-timbering has been added to the stuccoed gable.

Wright's house for inventor Harry C. Goodrich, at 534 North East Avenue, was the thirteenth commission for the Oak Park/River Forest area. Many of its features look forward to the Prairie house, including the predominance of geometric over historic design elements. The main entry is at the front, via a porch that has since been enclosed. The small vestibule is typical of Wright's compressed entrances. It opens into the large hall, sitting room, and library that span the front of the house. The tiled hearth in the sitting room has built-in seating and bookcases. Kitchen and dining room adjoin along the back, accessible by side and rear entries. The second-floor plan features five bedrooms and a bath opening from the hall at the head of the stairs.

Dark clapboard siding conceals a basement that is partly above ground level and extends to the level of the second-floor window sills. From here to the eaves, lighter siding links the windows, which are directly below the soffit. A dormer has been added to the slate roof on the street side, and awnings obscure the original windows, only one of which – next to the vestibule – is lead-camed. The Goodrich house may represent Wright's last use of clapboard siding, which he employed only for economic reasons.

In 1897 Wright received two commissions from stockbroker Warren Furbeck. Both houses were to be wedding gifts, the first to Furbeck's oldest son, George, the second to Rollin, the third of his five sons.

The George Furbeck house, constructed at 223 North Euclid Avenue, is notable for its use of the octagonal form, which Wright used extensively in his own studio, designed at about the same time. The lower facade was faced with brick, and the original porch has been enlarged and enclosed. The octagonal towers, inscribed within circles, stand on either side of the entry.

The main common space comprises an octagonal living room with a radius of 10 feet, 10 inches (equal to the tower diameter) and a 17-foot-deep dining room. Both rooms have fireplaces with alcove seating. Behind the dining room fireplace are the kitchen, laundry, and back porch. A single-story passage between kitchen and front door is lighted by a series of windows repeated in the north wall of the living room for maximum available light. The entry hall is flanked by the octagonal library in the south tower and the main stairwell in the north. The radiators are concealed by grillework, and the fireplaces are of Roman brick and oak.

Upstairs, the original master bedroom extended into the south tower with a dressing room adjacent to it. Four additional bedrooms and a bath opened off the central hallway, which has built-in seating at the head of the stairs. On the south end of the house, a third-floor dormer has been added to the broad hip roof. This intrusion on the design, along with the enclosure of the porch, have diminished the original sense of proportion. As built, the second story was shingled, but it was faced with brick when detailing of other features was simplified. The house has a strong presence, thanks in part to the prowlike forms of the exterior, which also

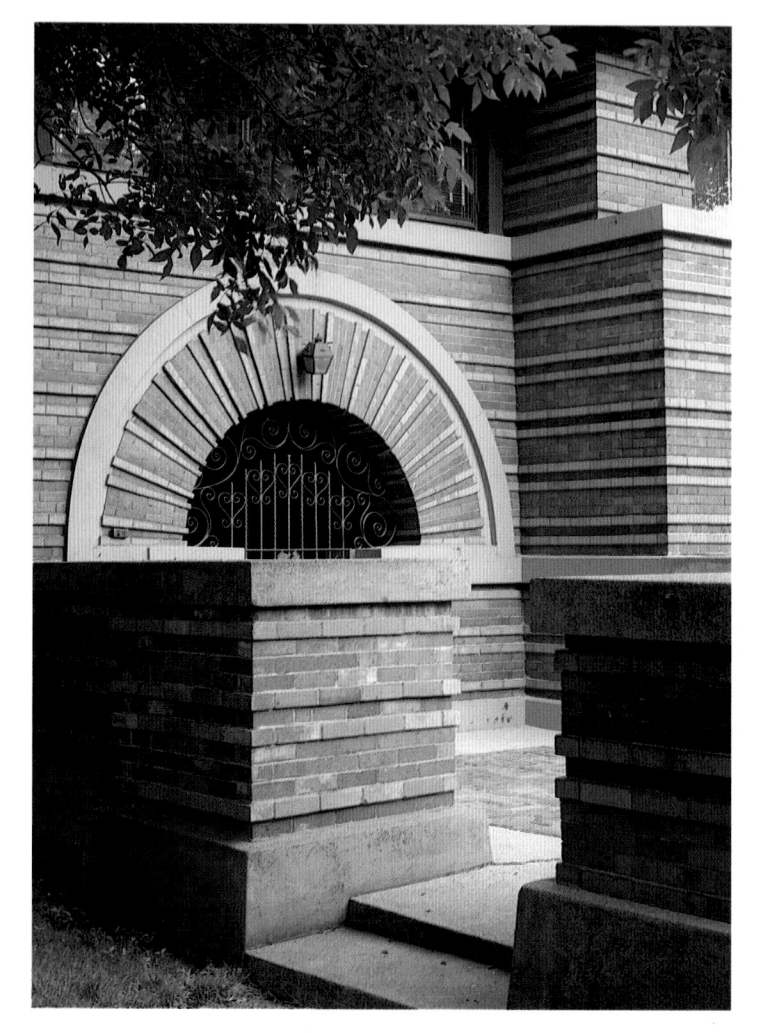

appear in the house designed for Rollin Furbeck at 515 Fair Oaks Avenue.

Built at a cost of $6,000, the three-story Rollin Furbeck house is laid out on a square plan with first-floor extensions: open front and rear porches and a porte cochere. Entry is from the semidetached front porch on the north side. Design features of note include the symmetrical treatment of the windows, broad hip roofs at varying heights, the first residential use of picture windows (in living and dining rooms), and a central mass three stories high with decorative plaster columns in the Sullivan style. Storrer describes the house as "a major transitional work from early square and rectangular plans, such as the 1896 Heller house, to the Prairie cruciform and pinwheel designs of the architect's first mature design period." (p. 40)

The surface of the lower floors runs to the sill of the floor above at both second- and third-story levels, with the pillars accenting the vertical thrust of the central mass. The rectangular living room extends the width of the house to the entry hall, which is flanked by a mez-zanine overlooking the entry porch. The fireplace is at the core of the house, and there is a sitting room adjacent to the back porch. The kitchen adjoins the large dining room, which opens to the porte cochere at the south end.

The second floor includes a master bedroom and bath with a generous closet and two smaller bedrooms at either side of the stairwell, with another bath. The third floor is notable for its cantilevered bedroom balcony, extending well beyond the second-floor exterior wall structural support. Apparently, this was Wright's first use of such cantilevering in domestic architecture. There is a second bedroom and a bath at this level – an unusually large allotment of space for servants' quarters at this time, although not unprecedented in Wright's plans, as, for example, in the Harry Goodrich and Walter Gale houses.

The residence was remodeled in 1907, possibly by Wright himself. At that time, the first floor was extended into the original rear porch to provide additional living space, and the porte cochere was enclosed.

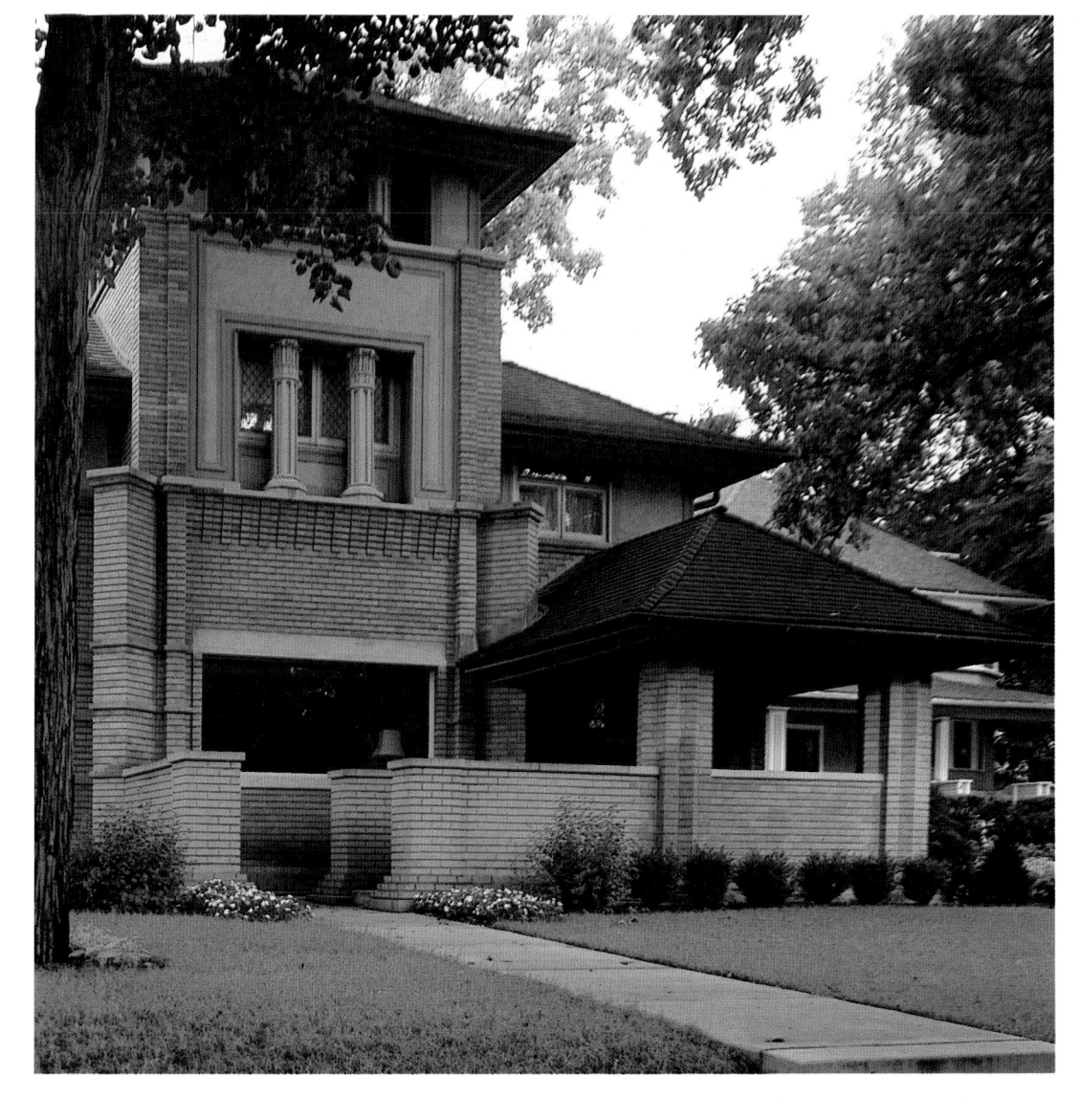

Left: The Rollin Furbeck house of 1897 has a three-story facade of tan brick with plaster columns and wood trim. The top-story windows are united to the overhanging eaves by a stucco band. The entrance is off-center, in the porch at right.

Opposite top: The Prairie vernacular is clear in the 1906 E.R. Hills-DeCaro house, remodeled by Wright from a Victorian structure dating to 1893. Horizontal surface banding, broad overhangs, and a steep multilevel roofline contribute to the strong presence of this house, which was occupied by its original owners and their family for 45 years.

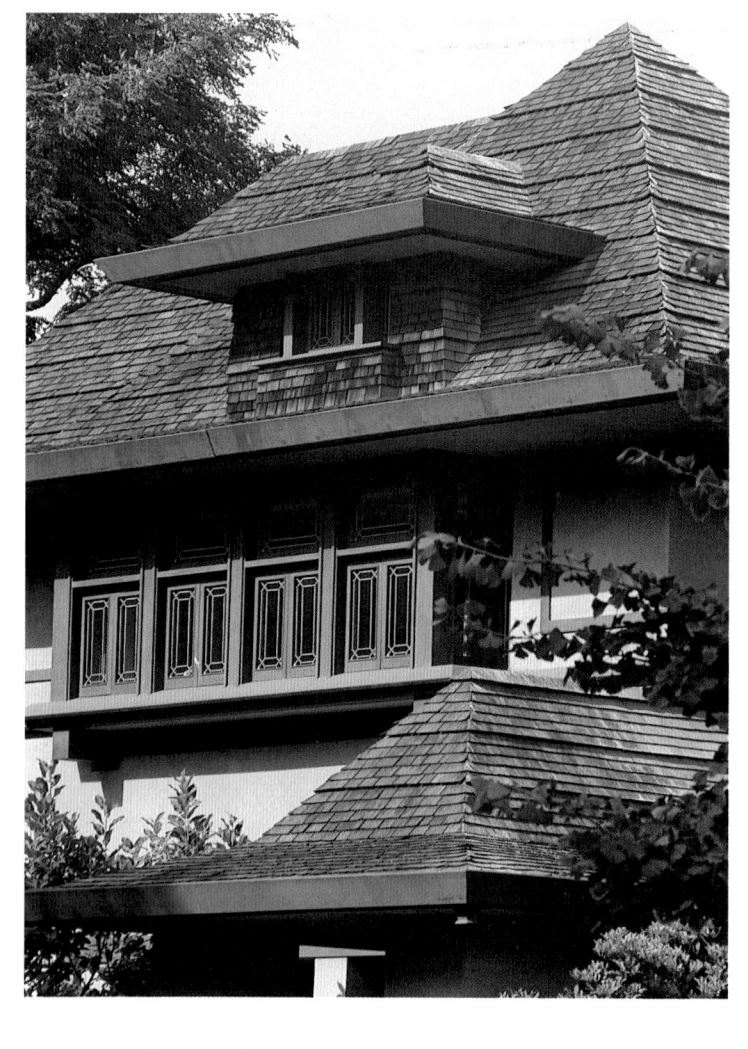

During the mid-1980s, restoration undertaken by architect John G. Thorpe included a new wood-shingled roof, copper leaders and gutters, and stripping of paint from exterior masonry. The projecting second-level open porch at the rear has been enclosed and supported.

The George W. Smith house, at 404 Home Avenue, has been considerably altered since its construction in 1898, and no plans are available for it. Japanese influence is suggested by the steeply pitched roof, originally covered with red-stained shingles, and the flaring eaves. The house itself was shingle-clad, although Wright was already employing horizontal board-and-batten siding (alternating boards with narrower strips of wood), which would become a feature of his Prairie houses and his later Usonian designs. The lower-level windows on the west side – double-hung sash – are unusually large, because the proximity of a neighboring house precluded living-room windows on the north wall. Three massive rectangular chimneys rise from the multilevel roof, giving the house a commanding presence.

Interior alterations have not been documented, but the conjectural plan for the original first floor shows a square design with a projecting entry porch (since enclosed) and a large bay window in the dining room. The vestibule opened to the sitting (living) room and to a central hall leading to the kitchen and dining room. The back porch projected from the kitchen. The stairwell adjoined the vestibule and led directly to the second-floor hall, which opened to four single bedrooms and a bath. The third floor was an attic.

Designed in 1896, three years after Wright left Alder & Sullivan to set up his own practice, the Smith house seems to look backward toward his association with Silsbee in the late 1880s rather than forward to the emergent Prairie style.

The Edward R. Hills home at 313 Forest Avenue began life as a Victorian dwelling one lot north of its present location. Built in 1883, it was purchased by Nathan Moore in 1900 and turned over to Wright for remodeling. The project was delayed until 1906 by legal problems. Then the house was moved to its present location and altered to Wright's design as a wedding gift to Moore's daughter Mary and her husband, attorney Edward R. Hills.

Entrance to the house is by way of a pinwheeled entry porch at the northeast corner leading into the central hallway. Adjacent to the entry is a long rectangular living room and library along the front of the house and a spacious dining room, family room, and kitchen to the rear. The mirrored dining-room sideboard, with display shelving, is unusually handsome, as is the stairwell, with its octagonal art-glass bay projecting from the north wall.

The second floor comprised two bedrooms, two baths, a study, and a porch off the central hallway, and the third floor had two bedrooms and a bath. The Hills family occupied the house for 45 years. After it fell into disrepair under subsequent owners, it was purchased by Tom and Irene DeCaro (1975) and carefully restored under the aegis of architect John D. Tilton. The Oak Park Landmark Commission renamed the restored building the Hills-DeCaro house in 1977.

Exterior banding, fenestration, and multilevel rooflines with broad overhanging eaves give the exterior a distinguished presence very different from the angular vertical thrust of the original structure. As reshaped by Wright, the house has a total of 136 windows.

The year 1901 brought Wright's work to national attention with publication by *The Ladies' Home Journal* of his perspective and plans for "A Home in a Prairie Town." That same year he designed the first Prairie-style house in Oak Park: the Frank W. Thomas house at 210 Forest Avenue. It was commissioned by James C.

Rogers as a gift for his daughter and son-in-law, the Frank Thomases.

The house had no excavated basement and no traditional attic - two features Wright deplored all his life and eventually eliminated from his designs. It is laid out on an L-shaped plan, with a ground floor containing servants' quarters and the main floor comprising the principal common and service spaces: living room with fireplace and book alcove, single-story dining room with breakfast alcove, kitchen, and pantries. The front entry is screened by walls on either side of the front walk leading to a Romanesque archway, reminiscent of Henry Hobson Richardson's designs and much used by Wright at this time. Inside, stairs ascend on the left to a landing, then rise in the opposite direction to a glassed-in breezeway. The effect is to bring the visitor from a compressed, almost claustrophobic environment into the brightness and space of the main level. The living room faces a long terrace and a porch that gives access to the back of the property. The rear entry is at the ground-floor level.

The stairwell to the top floor is at the rear of the house, and the bedrooms are in line, with a small balcony at either end. In 1922 a two-story addition, not visible from the street, was made by architects Thomas E. Tallmadge and Vernon S. Watson (members of the Prairie School, which Wright variously ignored and criticized as derivative of his own style). Originally surfaced with plaster, the house was shingled for many years until its restoration in 1975. The open second-floor veranda provides an unusual sense of privacy from the adjacent house and from the street. The self-contained appearance of the Thomas house, including the secluded archway entrance, earned it the local nickname "the Harem."

In 1902 friends and neighbors of Wright's, Arthur and Grace Heurtley, commissioned the handsome Prairie house at 318 Forest Avenue. It demonstrates Wright's mastery of his craft at the young age of thirty-five. Anchored to its site by a stylobate foundation, the Heurtley house rises to the second (main) floor sills in courses of tawny brick that alternately project and recede, forming a powerful horizontal dimension. The hip roof with central chimney overhangs the art-glass casement windows of the large main rooms: living room with fireplace and nearly continuous dining room with breakfast alcove (their combined area is more than a thousand square feet). A central corridor leads to the kitchen at one end and the fifty-two-foot-long veranda (now enclosed) at the other. Master and children's bedrooms and bath are at the back of the house, which is nearly square.

The first (ground) floor contains the entry hall, reached through an arch on the walled terrace, and

ample guest bedrooms with bath, servant's room, storage space, and playroom with fireplace opening to a veranda. The Heurtleys entertained often, and Wright provided them with a house ideal for party-giving, where he was a frequent guest himself. He also remodeled their summer cottage in northern Michigan.

The year 1902 was one of growth and innovation. Several commissions showed influences that Wright was always at pains to disavow, notably that of the Vienna Secessionists, who saw in the gifted young American architect a kindred spirit. Led by Josef Maria Olbrich, the Secessionists repudiated traditional styles of architecture in Munich, Berlin, and Vienna and embraced the rectilinear forms favored by such Scottish designers as Charles Rennie Mackintosh. International exhibitions and publications such as *The Studio* magazine kept artists on both sides of the Atlantic apprised of new design trends and ideologies.

The house built for William G. Fricke at 540 Fair Oaks Avenue was a collaboration with Webster Tomlinson and a forerunner of Wright's monolithic design for Unity Temple (Church). Its vertical massing suggests Secessionist influence at a period when Wright was moving closer to design principles in which horizontal emphasis was predominant. The overall plan for the Fricke house lacks clarity. It has a monumental quality that seems inappropriate to a private dwelling, like the Susan Lawrence Dana house at Springfield, Illinois, which would be remodeled – actually rebuilt – by Wright a year later.

Stucco on wood frame, the Fricke house has dark horizontal banding around the windows and a central mass that rises three stories to broad overhanging eaves, much like that of the Rollin Furbeck house. A semi-detached pavilion on the southeast side has been demolished.

The main entry brings one into the central hall at ground-floor level. To the left, the reception-room bay projects from the facade. To the right is the large living room with fireplace; its bay overlooks the side of the property. A long rectangular dining room opposite the living room originally had a view of the pavilion and the garden. Pantry and kitchen adjoin the dining room, and a porch at the north side faces the garage, commissioned by the house's second owner, Emma Martin, in 1907. The two-story garage that Wright added contains a single upstairs room with fireplace.

The second floor rooms, grouped clockwise around the stairwell, include four bedrooms, two with balconies and the largest with a fireplace and veranda; a bath; and a maid's room. The third floor was designed as a large billiards room with fireplace. Much of the furniture was built in to Wright's specifications, and detailing throughout is unmistakably his work.

There is a superficial resemblance between the Fricke house and the one designed for Chicago businessman William E. Martin in 1902, but the Martin house is more attractive and closer to the Prairie house aesthetic in its realization. It too was built on three levels, but the horizontal quality is enhanced by long wings on the ground floor and by extending both trim and windows around the corners of the house. Spacious

Opposite top: Perspective of "A Home in a Prairie Town," which attracted national attention when it was published in *The Ladies' Home Journal* in 1901. Its influence on suburban house design would be apparent for decades to come.

Right: In Europe, Wright's work was compared to that of the Vienna Secessionists, notably Josef Maria Olbrich, as seen in a project drawing for Hochzeitsturm (1907-08).

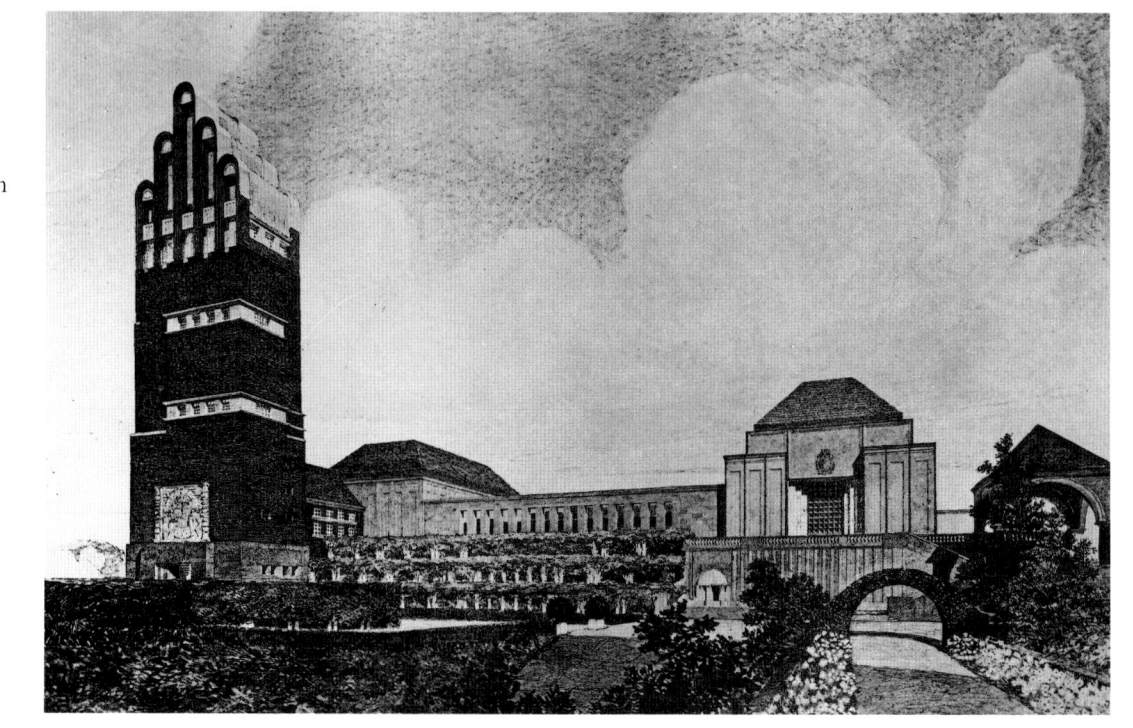

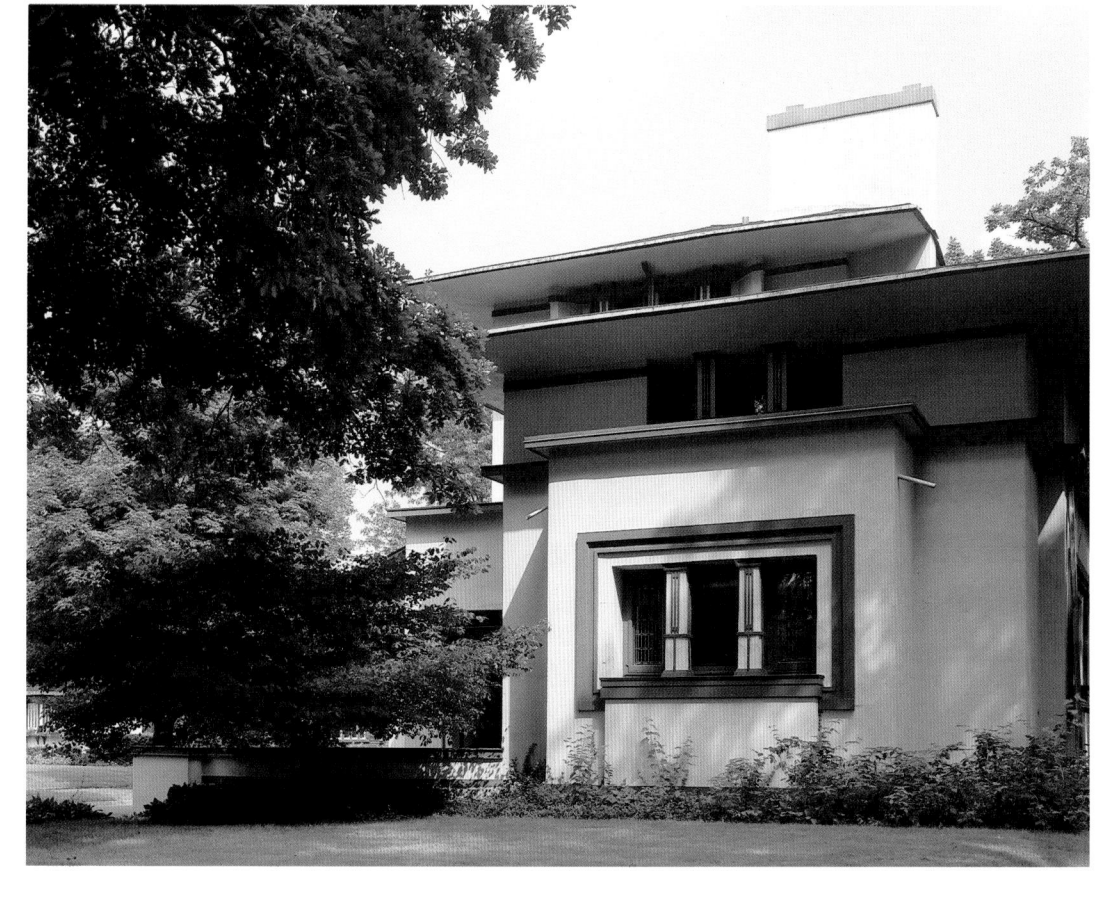

Left: Fenestration of the three-story William G. Fricke house (1901), with its dark banding against plaster walls, is in the Prairie style. The stylobate foundation is partially obscured by foliage.

Below: Wright's Larkin Administration Building in Buffalo, New York, broke new ground in commercial architecture, with its top-lighted atrium, advanced ventilation system, and custom-built furniture and fixtures.

Opposite: The stately Prairie house for Buffalo client Darwin D. Martin (1904) featured bands of art-glass casement windows, low piers surmounted by pedestaled urns, and light-colored soffits under the broad eaves, which reflected light to the interior.

and impressive, but not overpowering, the Martin house made maximum use of its large level lot at 636 North East Avenue. In 1909 the property was enhanced by a wooden pergola joined to one of the porches, with gardens on either side, pools, bridges, and a lawn tennis court. Landscape design was by Wright's colleague Walter Burley Griffin, who had supervised construction of the house, and who would soon marry Marion Mahony, the second woman to graduate from the Massachusetts Institute of Technology with a degree in architecture. Unfortunately, most of the landscaping has disappeared.

The front entry opened to both the hall and the veranda. Principal activities spaces on the first floor included a library, terrace, open porch, and living room with a deep fireplace alcove. The long hallway is lighted by an art-glass skylight, and there is wood paneling and built-in furniture throughout. The dining room overlooked the garden, and a maid's room adjoined the kitchen.

On the second-floor plan, four bedrooms and a bath opened from the central hallway at the head of the stairs, the largest bedroom with a dressing room and balcony overlooking the west side of the grounds. The third floor consisted of a playroom with balcony and decks, a servant's room, and several closets.

William E. Martin cooperated closely with Wright

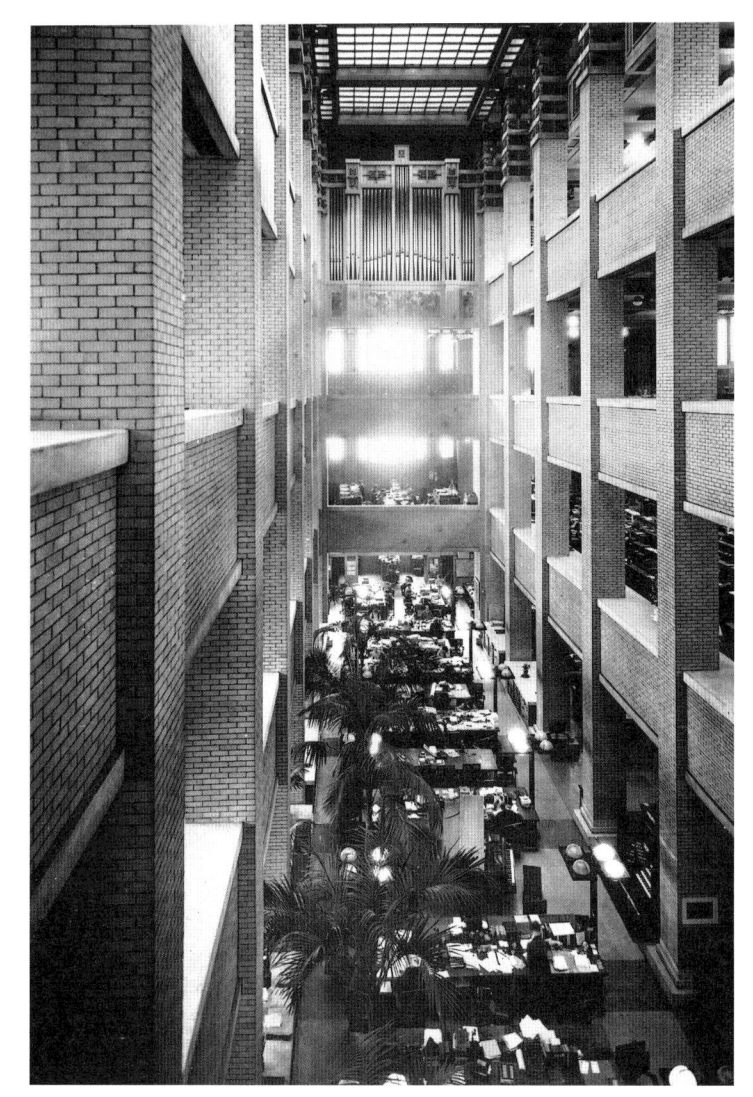

highly educated and polished, but no dude – a straight-type of manhood. He is not a freak – not a 'crank' – hair (bushy, not long), about 32 years old. A splendid athletic-looking young man of medium build, black even skeptical, tough-minded businessmen:'"He is an impression of the charismatic quality that won over astic letter about Wright to his brother Darwin gives an all in Buffalo, New York. William E. Martin's enthusi-Heath house and the Larkin Administration Building, including the Darwin D. Martin house, the W. R. Martin resulted in a total of nine major commissions, downtown Chicago). Wright's relationship with Wright's design for Martin's E-Z Polish factory in the result (although the two quarreled vehemently over on every aspect of the project and was very happy with

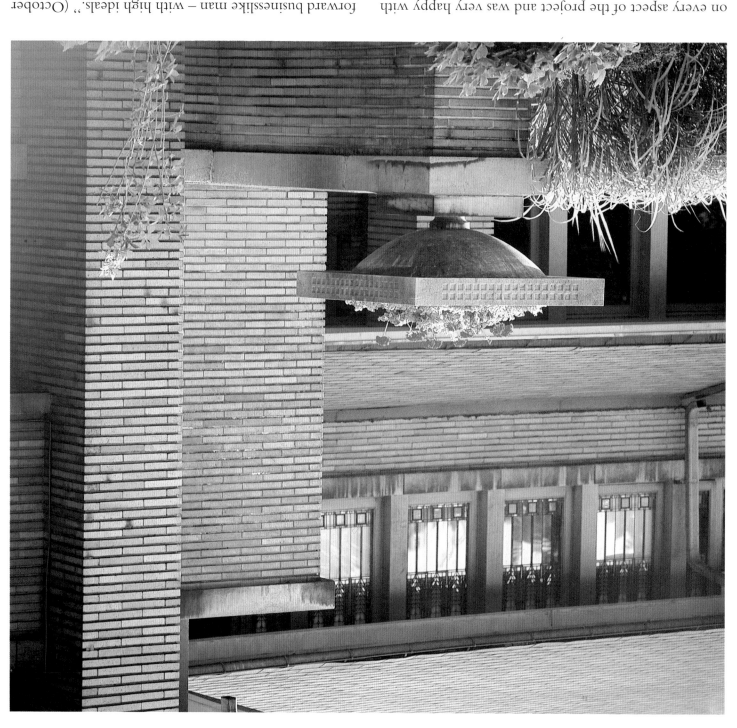

forward businesslike man – with high ideals.'" (October 2, 1902). In time, Darwin D. Martin would become one of Wright's best friends and supporters – and, often, a peacemaker between his volatile brother William and their equally demanding architect.

The house Wright designed for Edwin H. Cheney and his wife, Mamah Borthwick Cheney, in 1904 was both a personal and professional landmark in his career. Located at 520 North East Avenue, it appears to be only one story high, but the "basement" is really a lower level, lighted by windows with sills at ground level (invisible from the street because of the retaining wall). It was designed to include a two-car garage, but the Oak Park city council refused approval of this use because of possible fire from gasoline fumes, so most of

the space became a separate apartment for Mrs. Cheney's sister. The rest of the lower level contained storage space, laundry facilities, and a servant's room and bath.

The main-level entry on the south side is entirely hidden from the street. The visitor follows a circuitous garden path to a series of steps leading up to the small entrance. The exterior is of brick with wood trim, and the hip roof is low-pitched, surmounted by a single massive chimney. Beside it, a skylight admits light through the unfinished attic space into a central corridor between the four bedrooms and two baths at the rear and the long flow of living space along the front: dining room, living room, and library. The perimeter walls and terraces give this Prairie house a strong sense of enclosure and privacy — a quality that would become increasingly prominent in Wright's work. The main floor has a total of fifty-two windows, all of iridescent art glass. Other noteworthy features include the dining-room sideboard; the lighting fixtures, designed for gas or electricity; and concealed radiators throughout. A board-and-batten garage was added to the property in 1910, and renovation was undertaken in 1965 and 1968 after damage by fires.

The Cheneys, married in 1899, had adopted an orphaned niece in 1901, and their son and daughter were born within the next four years. Their house was designed to be what Wright called ''a good-time place,'' but the relationship that grew up between him and Mamah Cheney would eventually result in the break-up of both families. Their affair was common knowledge before their abrupt departure for Europe in 1909. They spent almost two years abroad: in Germany, where Wright worked with publisher Ernst Wasmuth on a monograph of his work, and in Italy. When they returned to the United States they settled at Taliesin, the famous country house and studio Wright built in Spring Green, Wisconsin.

In 1904, the same year he designed the Cheney house, Wright planned a house he would describe as ''the progenitor of Fallingwater.'' Unbuilt until 1909, the house designed for Laura R. Gale is a flat-roofed, two-story residence of cantilever plan at 6 Elizabeth Court. Laura Gale had been widowed in 1907, and Wright's second home for her was built while she and her children were at their summer cottage in Michigan. It would remain in the family until 1943. The links to Fallingwater are seen in the use of open interior space, corner windows, and the projecting bedrooms of the second floor. Originally planned as a concrete structure,

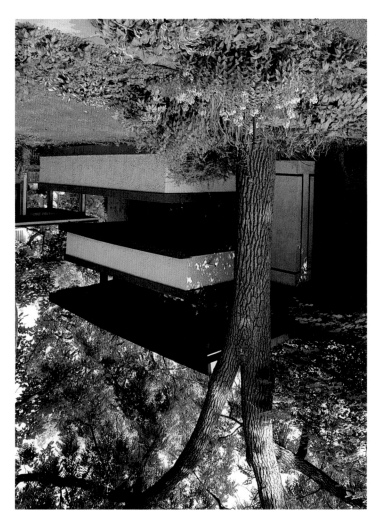

it was built of stucco and wood. The main floor includes a large living room with brick fireplace, behind which is the main hallway leading to the stairs. The dining room is set off from the living room by a two-step rise and built-in cabinets, and the kitchen adjoins it. The main entry is characteristically enclosed, and the terrace runs the width of the living room. Upstairs, a cantilevered balcony extends from adjacent bedrooms to overhang the terrace. Two additional bedrooms, a maid's room, and a bath are part of the layout.

Extensive restoration was done during the 1960s, and architect John Thorpe carried out the restoration of 1984–5. At this time the basement, formerly unfinished, was converted into a playroom.

In 1904 the Unitarian church in Oak Park, to which the Wrights belonged, was destroyed by fire and Wright was invited to design a new building for the congregation. The result was Unity Temple, a flat-roofed monolithic structure of reinforced concrete at 875 Lake Street that became a landmark in ecclesiastical architecture. It was designed on three levels, comprising worship space, social and educational facilities (Unity House), and a central entry hall separating the two.

were prepared by Barry Byrne before he left Wright's office to open his own architectural practice. Restoration of the building was undertaken in 1961, and it has been designated one of seventeen American buildings designed by Wright to be retained as an example of his architectural contribution to American culture.

Like the Edward R. Hills house, the 1906 Beachy house, at 238 Forest Avenue, is a total remodeling. It was originally a Gothic-style cottage on the same extensive property. The yard measures 133 by 330 feet, and the building is placed at the north lot line, with maximum available sunlight. Its horizontal plan, with projecting porches, makes it look even larger than it is. The

The use of poured concrete as the building material was radically new. It forms all the exterior walls and ornamentation, with the coarse aggregate showing through. The successive pours of the concrete are visible in the layers that ascend from the stylobate foundation to the columns framing art-glass clerestory windows. Massive towers at each corner confirm the monumental quality.

The restrained elegance of the worship space is delineated by horizontal and vertical moldings and by lighting fixtures that alternate spheres and cubes like those of the plan itself – a Greek cross in a square. Pews at three levels give a sense of enclosure and relatedness to the speaker at the pulpit. The working drawings

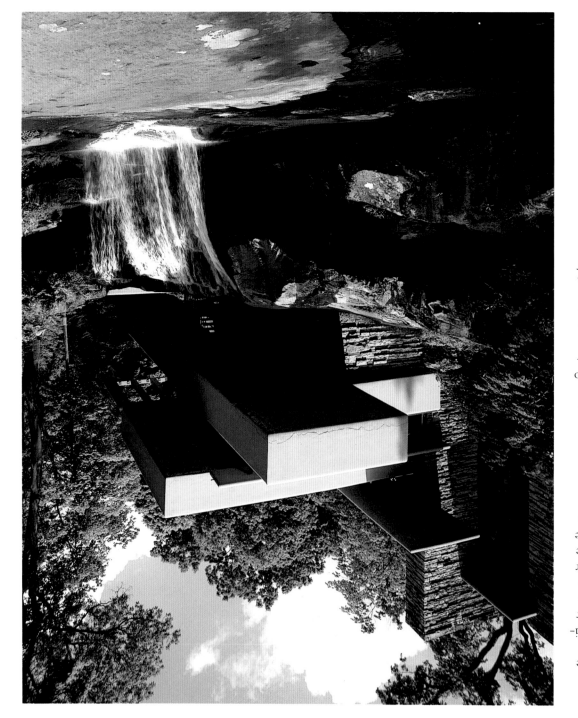

Opposite top: The house designed for Laura Gale in 1904 has been described as the forerunner of Wright's best-known work, Fallingwater, primarily because of its cantilever plan, with the projecting bedrooms of the second floor jutting out over the ground-floor rooms and terraces. The house was intended to be of concrete construction, but as built, five years after design, it was surfaced in plaster with wood trim.

Right: Fallingwater (1935), built for Edgar J. Kaufmann, Sr., over a stream in the western Pennsylvania highlands, took the cantilever principle to new heights. Reinforced-concrete slabs anchored to the native rock formations carried the house out over the stream that was the focal point of the wooded site. Corner windows gave an uninterrupted view of the natural surroundings. The house has been called "the apotheosis of the horizontal."

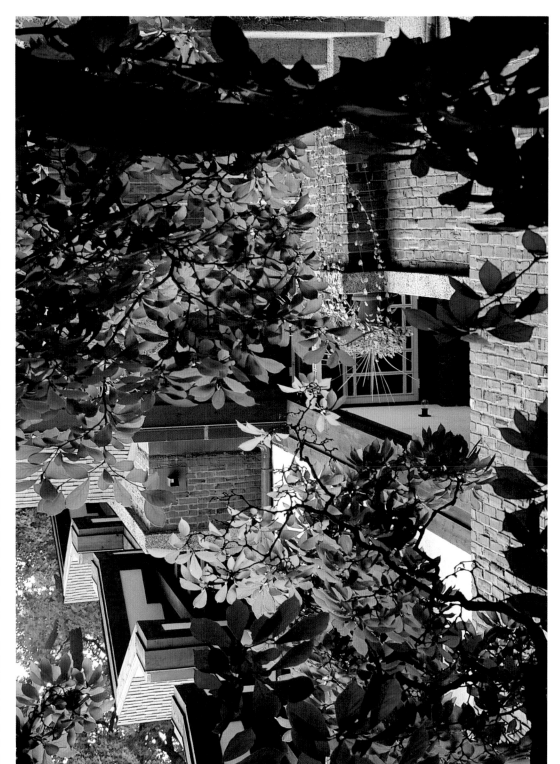

Left: The handsome Beachy residence (1906) began life as a Gothic-style cottage that was transformed into a substantial Prairie house of brick with plaster and wood trim. Mature plantings on this very large lot enhance the scene.

Opposite right: A replica of the original Scoville Park Fountain on Lake Street, designed by Wright in 1903 with sculpture by his frequent collaborator Richard Bock, who con- tributed to many projects of this period, including the Frank Lloyd Wright Home and Studio.

Opposite left: The design for Unity Temple was a radical departure from ecclesiastical architecture as the Middle West had known it prior to 1904. Wright's use of poured concrete for the monolithic structure pioneered the use of this material in the United States. Properly called Unity Church, it comprises a worship space for a congregation of 400 and a parish house for social and educational use. Barry Byrne prepared the working drawings.

massing of masonry is typical of the Prairie house, with broad bands of stonework and windows overhung by broad-eaved rooflines at both levels.

The main entry is concealed on the north wall. The rectangular living room overlooks the side yard and a porch and has a fireplace of dark-red hand-formed Roman brick. Both the fireplaces – the other is upstairs – have mortar joints at thirds, adding interest to the sur- face of the brickwork. A large dining room with break- fast alcove overlooks the veranda, flanked by loggias. The central hall contains the stairwell and narrows to a

corridor giving access to the coatroom, with half-bath; the kitchen; and the maid's room and bath. Wright- designed fixtures and furniture of cherry wood have been preserved. A variety of structural woods adds warmth and interest: redwood for the roof framing, structural members, and partitions; oak for the window frames, stringcourses, and flooring; and cedar for the beams supporting the porch.

The second floor has four large bedrooms, two baths, and ample closets for clothes and linen storage. The original tile roof has been replaced, and the dam-

house Wright designed for Balch in 1911 remains, at

Japanese prints.) The shop no longer stands, but the trip that Wright began his extensive collection of with his client Ward Willits and his wife. (It was on this showed the influence of Wright's visit to Japan in 1905 & Balch, on Oak Park's Lake Street. The design the remodeling of his interior decorators' shop, Pebbles Wright had worked with Oscar B. Balch in 1907 on floor remained largely as built in 1875.

porch. The stairwell was redesigned, but the second and doors for the dining room, which opened to a fireplace was remodeled, and Wright designed furniture traves to achieve a horizontal quality. The living room eleven-foot ceilings, with stringcourses replacing archi- spaces that flowed into one another under the original tially altered. Its boxlike rooms were broken down into not carried out, but the first-floor interior was substan- (1909). Many of Wright's plans for the building were William H. Copeland residence at 400 Forest Avenue Another remodeling commission was that for the working drawings.

age caused by a 1990 fire was repaired based on original

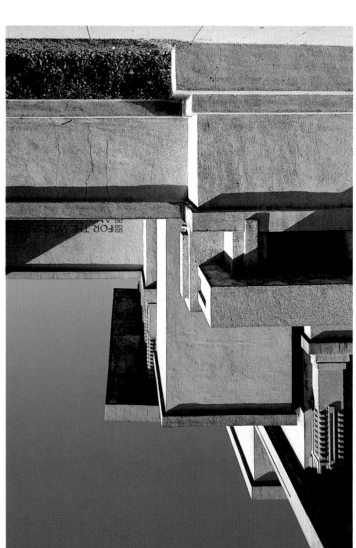

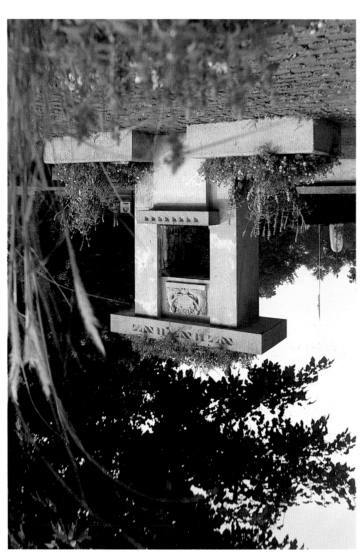

remodeling of the kitchen and exterior design elements. of the Balch house was undertaken in 1991, with some windows, as in many designs of this period. Renovation ters. The roof is flat and projects over bands of casement baths, and a dressing room comprise the upstairs quar- these have long been enclosed. Five bedrooms, two The second floor originally had four balconies, but almost surround the structure.

cealed, and a high-walled terrace and security wall usual in the Balch house. The entrance is entirely con- concern with privacy is even more pronounced than brick, centrally located in the living room. Wright's place is typical of designs from this period: tan Roman that most of the fifty windows are of this type. The fire- that worked to bring the outside in, is seen in the fact decided preference for casement windows, a feature ceiling lights, a china cabinet, and a sideboard. Wright's activities spaces include built-in bookshelves, art-glass ing room on either side. Wright fixtures in the main overlooking the terrace framed by the library and din- is on a symmetrical axis, with the long living room 611 North Kenilworth Avenue. Atypically, the design

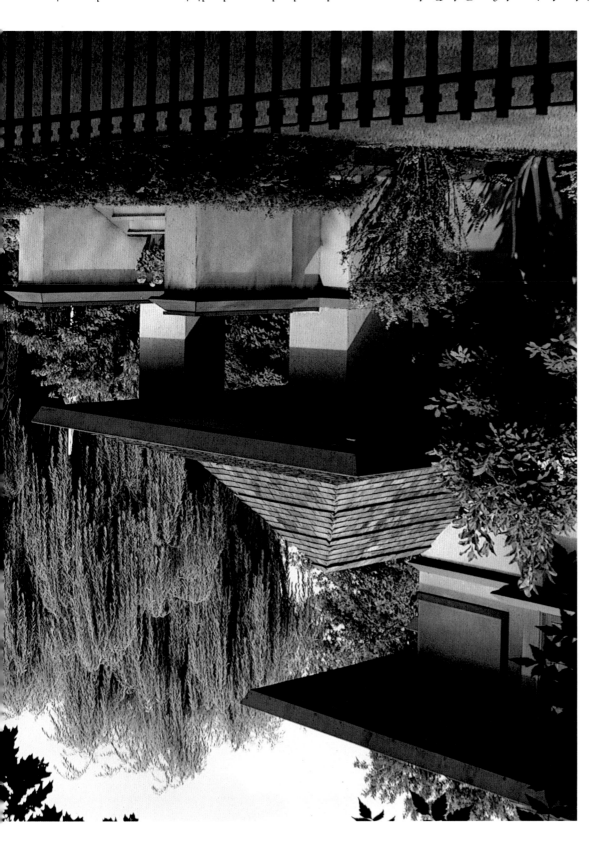

porte cochere leads past the living room to the main entry. To the right of the entrance is a large dining room with kitchen, washroom, and pantry behind. A breakfast porch (now enclosed) projects into the back. Upstairs, a former sewing room has been taken into the master bedroom suite, and two of the three small baths have been enlarged into one. Three other bedrooms and a balcony over the breakfast porch complete the second level under its low hipped roof.

The last house that Wright designed for Oak Park (1913) was that of physician Harry S. Adams and his wife, at 710 Augusta Avenue. The final plan (after numerous revisions to the original design could not be agreed upon) was a clear statement of the Prairie house ideal. The two-story brick house, seventy feet long, has limestone bands at both sill levels and a long veranda and porte cochere at one end, emphasizing the horizontal lines of the house. A sheltered walkway from the

Right: The serene beauty of Oak Park is exemplified in this photograph of the E.R. Hills-DeCaro (left) and Nathan G. Moore houses from Forest Avenue.

Wright's masterful treatment of the interior – art-glass windows, furniture, moldings, fireplace surround and copper lighting fixtures – is especially notable in view of the fact that he was turning at this time to new ideas and objectives. Now more than forty years old, he had made a decisive break with his past when he left for Europe in 1909. New paths had taken him to Taliesin East, in his ancestral Wisconsin, had surrounded him with new apprentices (some call them disciples), and

had opened the way to the textile-block house, Fallingwater, the Usonian style, and all the later devel-opments of his long career. His buildings still speak to us more strongly than the many books he wrote about them, and they speak in a uniquely American idiom. It is precisely in their richness and variety, constantly evolving into something fresh and unexpected, that we find the quality that makes Frank Lloyd Wright pre-eminent among American architects.

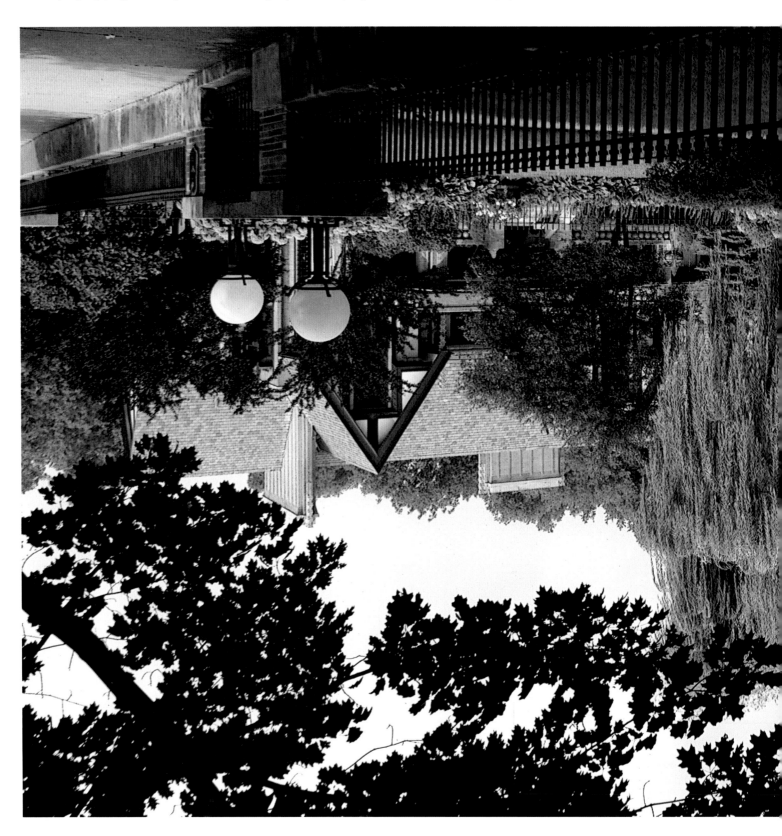

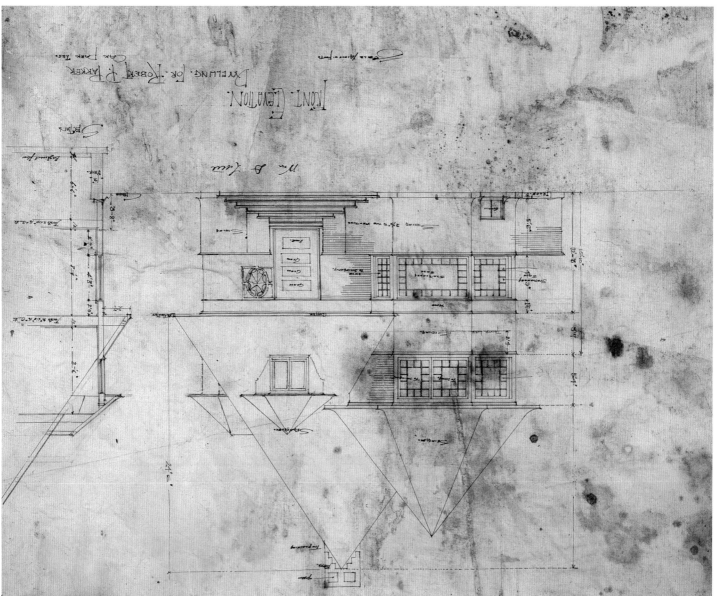

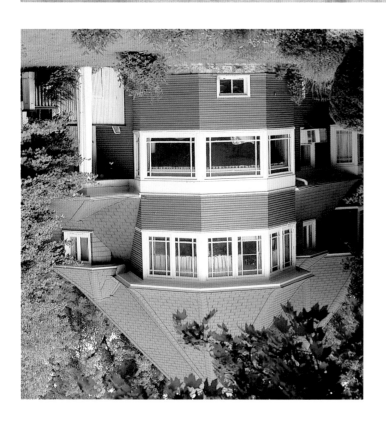

Robert P. Parker House, 1892
1019 West Chicago Avenue

Thomas H. Gale House, 1892
1027 West Chicago Avenue

Right: The Robert P. Parker house was commissioned together with the Thomas H. Gale House and they were based on the same T plan. Designed during Wright's tenure with Adler & Sullivan, the Parker house is in the Queen Anne style but with some key differences. The Queen Anne style was popular in the United States from the Philadelphia Centennial Exhibition of 1876 until the turn of the century. It emphasized domestic comfort, visual interest and livability.

Below: The plan of the Parker house illustrates the important alterations that Wright made to the Queen Anne with his use of octagons and squares and pronounced steep rooflines that project out from the building, adding an increased sense of shelter. These alterations offer a glimpse of Wright's future work. *The Frank Lloyd Wright Archives, © The Frank Lloyd Wright Foundation.*

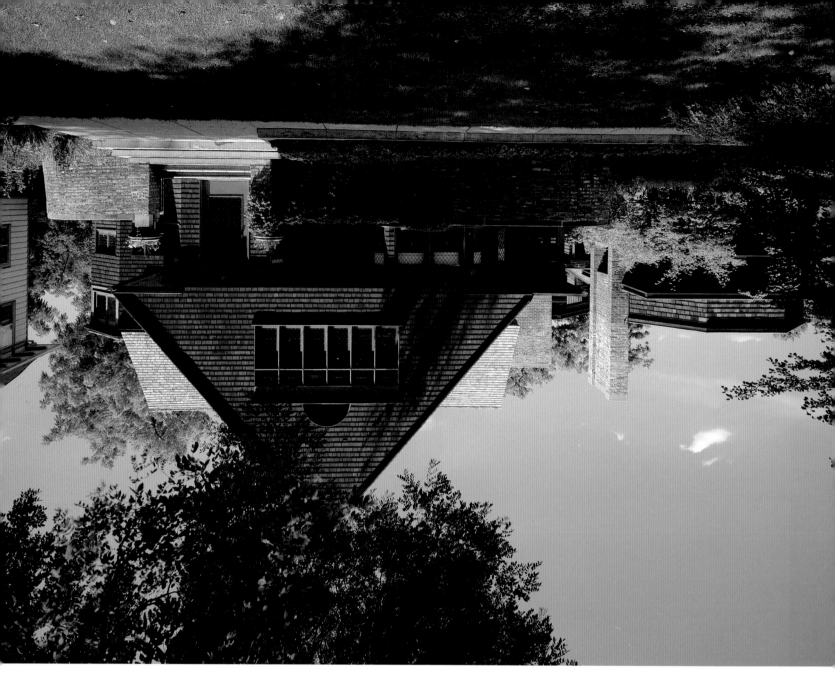

Frank Lloyd Wright Home and Studio, 1889-1911

951 West Chicago Avenue

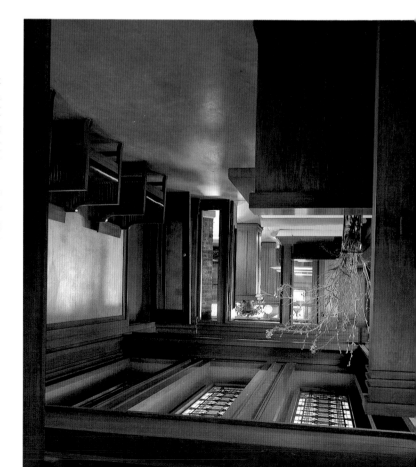

Left: The gracious sky-lighted entry to the Frank Lloyd Wright Studio, which must have inspired confidence in prospective clients through its skillful melding of rich woodwork, art and clear glass, and burnished surfaces glowing with light.

Below: The Frank Lloyd Wright Residence is the oldest extant house by Wright and shows the influence of the Shingle style in its steeply gabled roof and row of casement windows. Especially popular on the New England coast, the style was influenced by the work of British architect Richard Norman Shaw, developed for the United States by Henry Hobson Richardson in the 1880s.

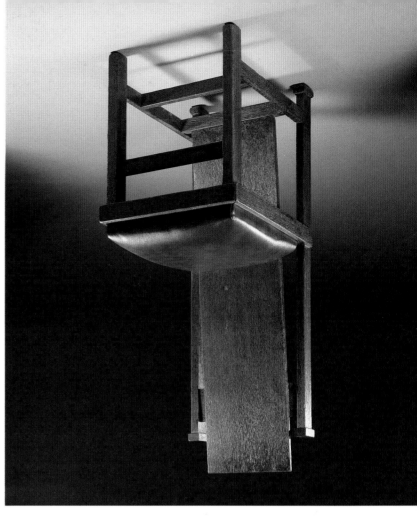

Above: The north facade of the Wright Home and Studio shows the remarkable difference in design of the studio, with its lower profile, deeply shadowed areas, and disparate geometric forms in shingles and brick.

Left: With his home as a design workshop, Wright was free to follow his preferred method of designing all furniture and fixtures for his buildings. Side chair, 1904. Oak, leather upholstery, 40¼" H × 15" W × 18¾" D. Gift of The Sydney and Frances Lewis Foundation, Virginia Museum of Fine Arts, Richmond, VA (85.74).

Right: The elegant lighting grid over the dining room table enhances the sense of the communal space for sharing meals as "a room within a room." The high-backed chairs contribute to the feeling of enclosure.

Far right: The inglenook was a feature popularized by the Arts and Crafts Movement, which had a strong influence on Wright's early design period. The concept of the fireplace as "the heart of the house" would be carried through as floor plans became more open and the hearth served as both focal point and screen between one living space and another.

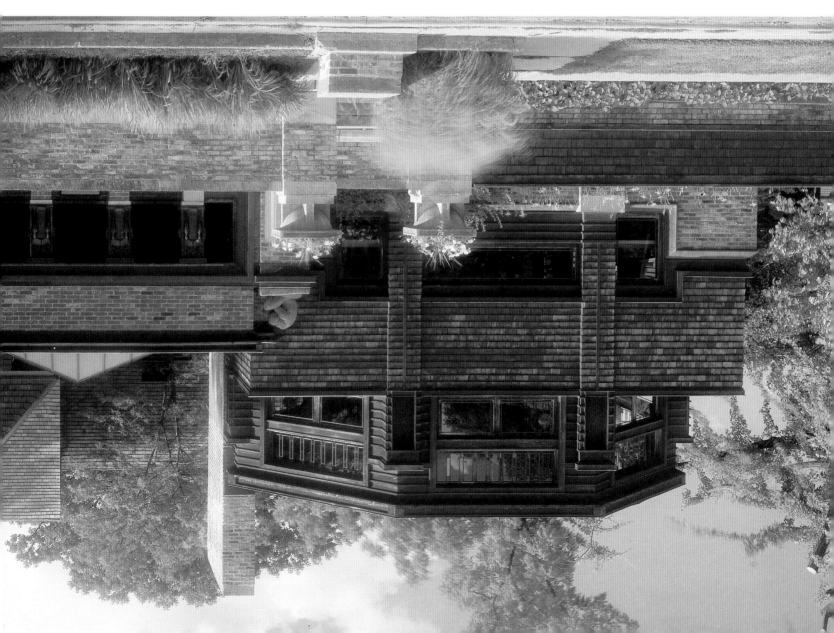

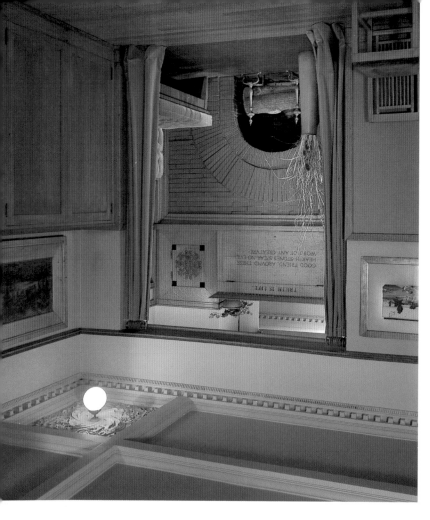
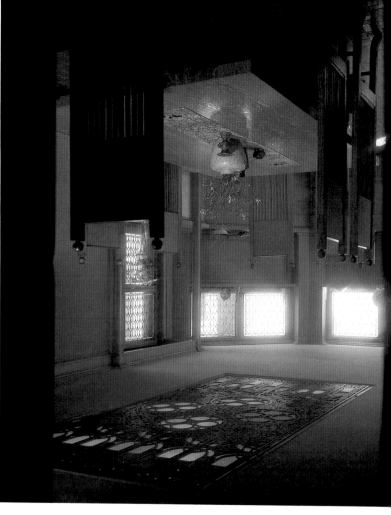
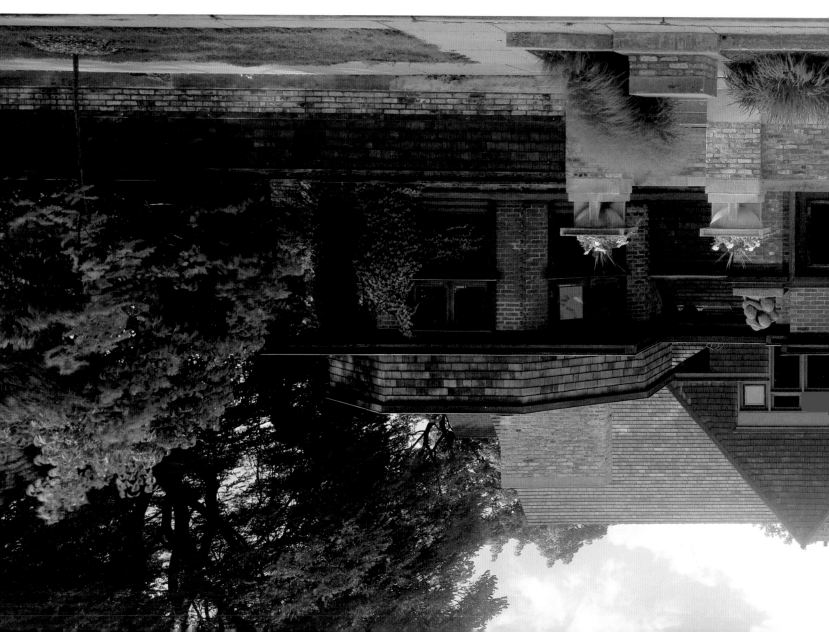

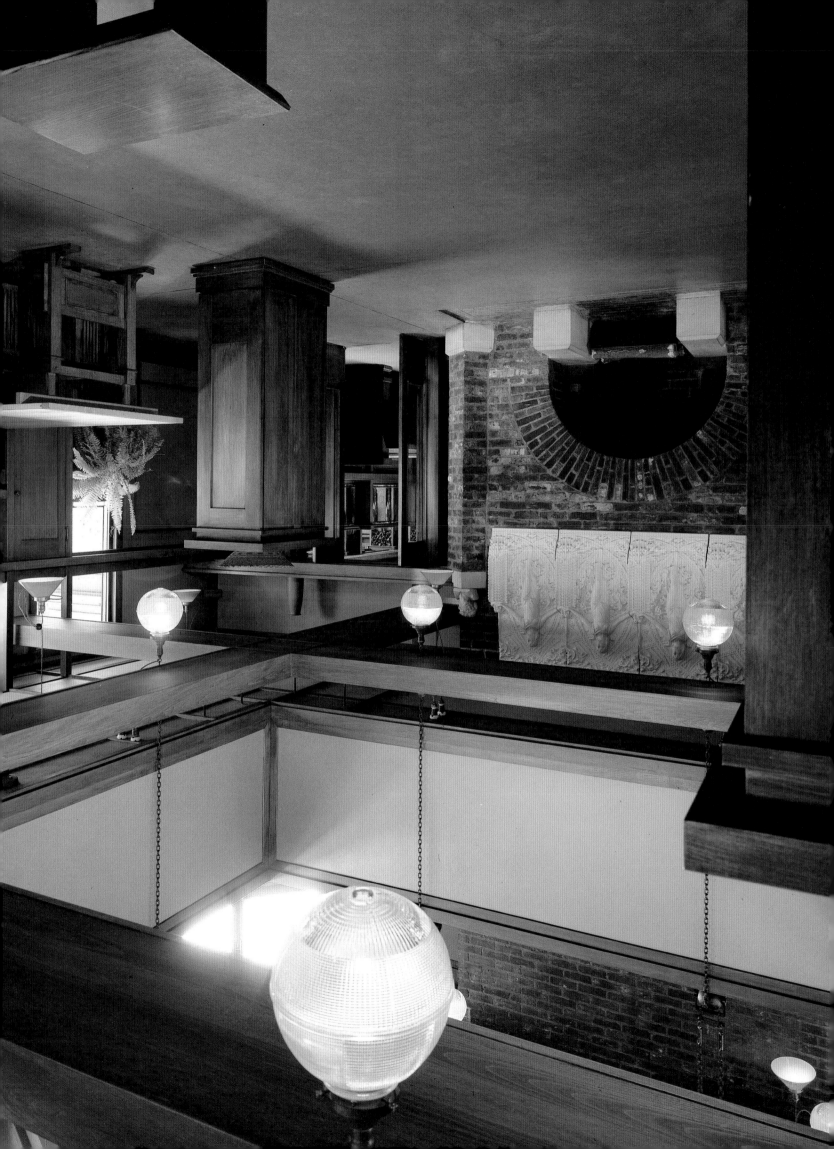

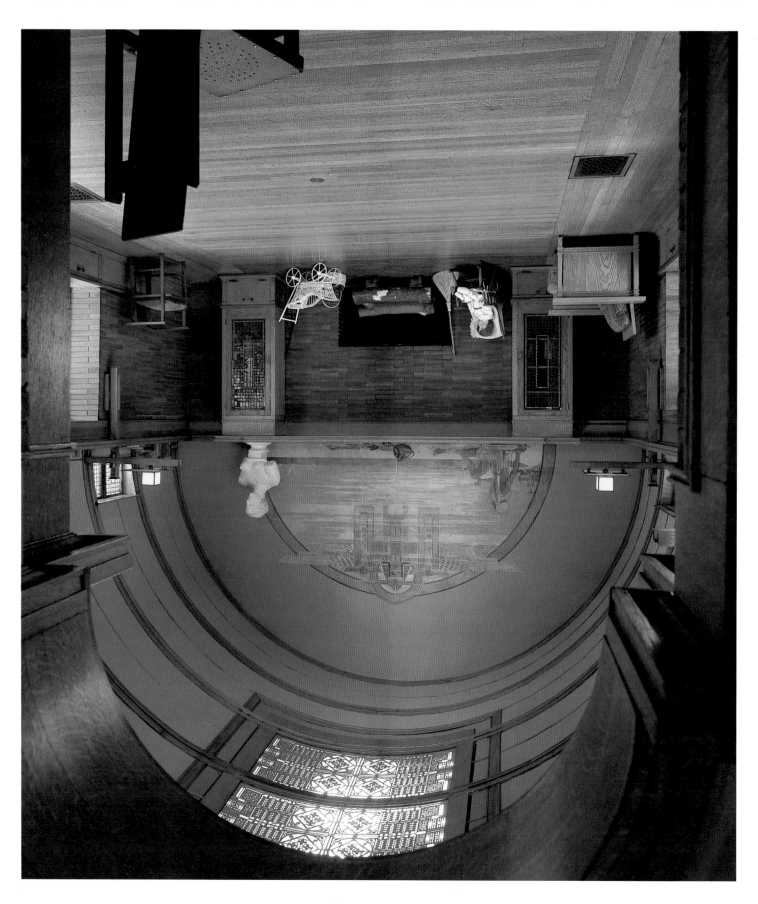

Opposite: The two-story drafting room in the Wright Studio, lighted by clerestory windows and fixtures of Wright's design. Spatial elements, including the balcony, are defined by string-courses. The frieze above the fireplace is reminiscent of Sullivan.

Above: The striking barrel-vaulted playroom added to the Wright residence in 1893 has a fireplace surround of narrow-gauge Roman brick with built-in shelving and brick wainscoting carried into the window embrasures. The arch of the mural echoes the soaring vaulted ceiling.

FRANK LLOYD WRIGHT HOME AND STUDIO

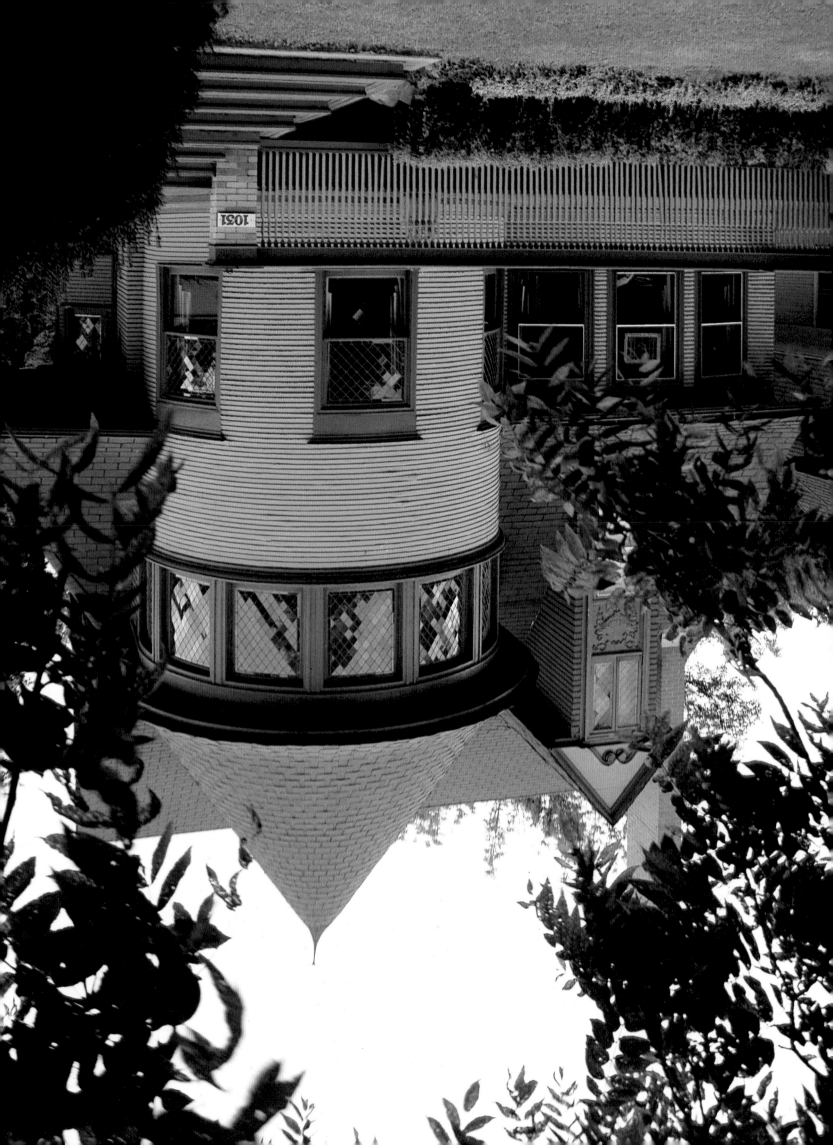

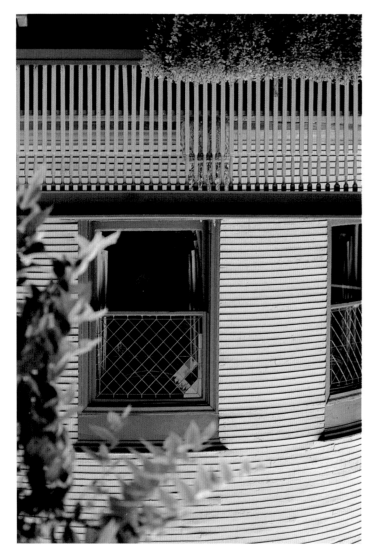

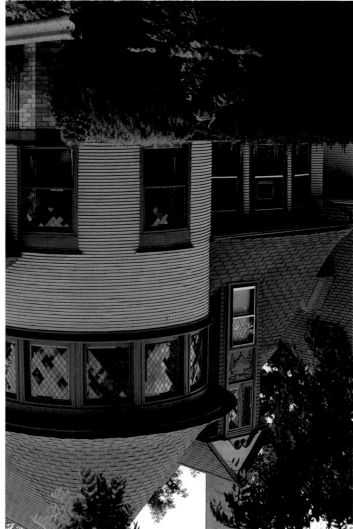

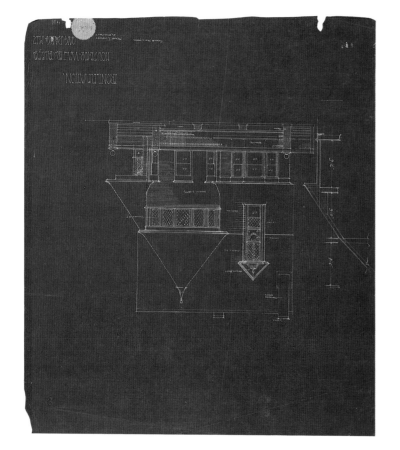

Walter Gale House, 1893

1031 West Chicago Avenue

Opposite: The Walter Gale house appears much as it did in 1893, with pleasing asymmetry provided by the Queen Anne-style turret with its diamond-paned casement windows and the tall, narrow dormer facing the front. The ground-floor windows are double-hung sash.

Right: Front elevation of the Walter Gale house showing the front terrace, demolished at one time but now restored. *The Frank Lloyd Wright Archives,* © *The Frank Lloyd Wright Foundation.*

Below: Detail of the clapboard turret with its conical peaked roof and the decorative panel above the two-story dormer.

Bottom right: The vertical lines of the balustrade form a counterpoint to the horizontal clapboards and the diamond-shaped panes of the mullioned windows.

Francis J. Woolley House, 1893
1030 West Superior Street

Nathan G. Moore House, 1895
(remodeled 1923)
333 North Forest Avenue

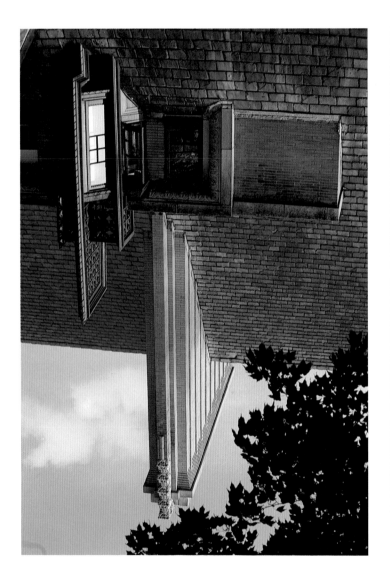

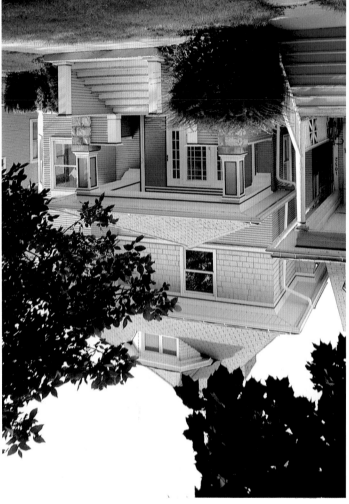

Above: The conventional but pleasing Woolley house includes an entry porch with low walls on either side of the steps and decorative square pillars. The front door is framed by multipaned clear-glass windows of equal height, and the uneven roofline, ascending from entry porch to third-story gable in the steeply sloped main roof, adds interest.

Above right: The Nathan G. Moore house is a flight of eclectic fancy, with its massive horizontal chimney and projecting windows set into pierced screens in the Japanese mode. The original tile roof was replaced by slate after the fire of 1922.

Opposite top: Tudor Revival elements of the Moore house include steeply pitched roofs, vertical half-timbering, pitched-roof dormers, intersecting gables, and the stone balustrade along the atypical porch.

Opposite bottom: The original south elevation of the Moore house, showing the Tudor-style stacked chimney and the horizontal half-timbering that was subsequently eliminated. *The Frank Lloyd Wright Archives, © The Frank Lloyd Wright Foundation.*

SOVTH ELEVATION
RESIDENCE FOR N·G·MOORE ESQ.
OAK PARK ILL.
FRANK L·WRIGHT ARCHITECT

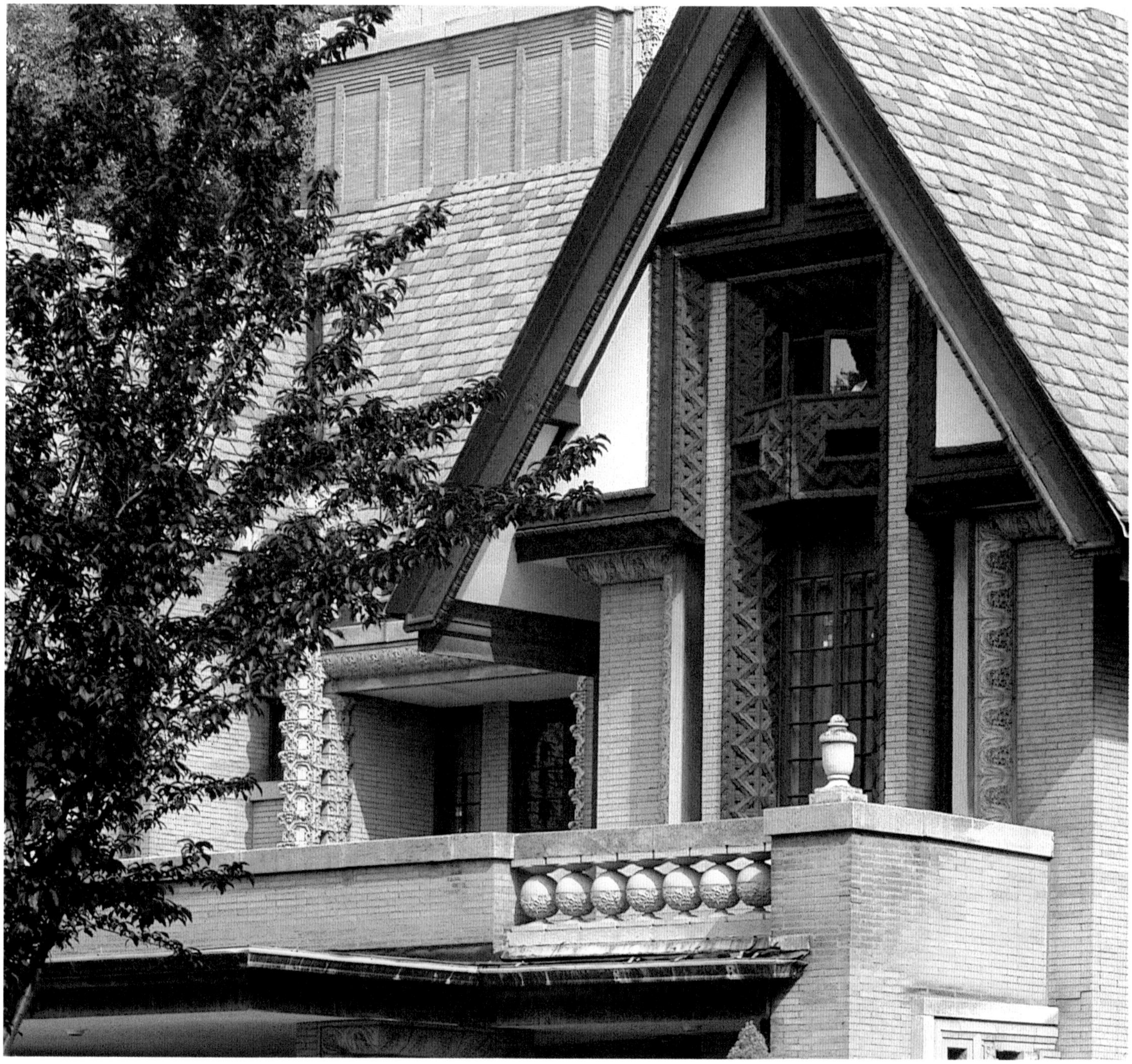

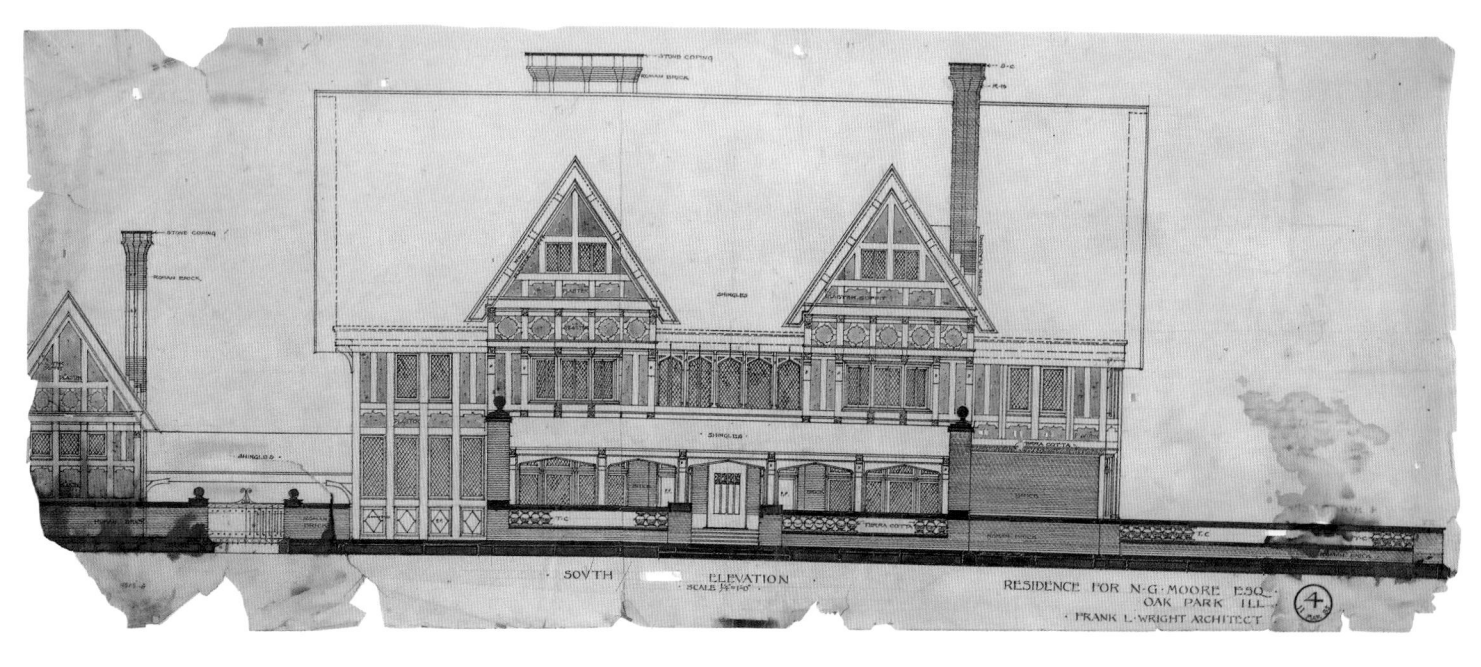

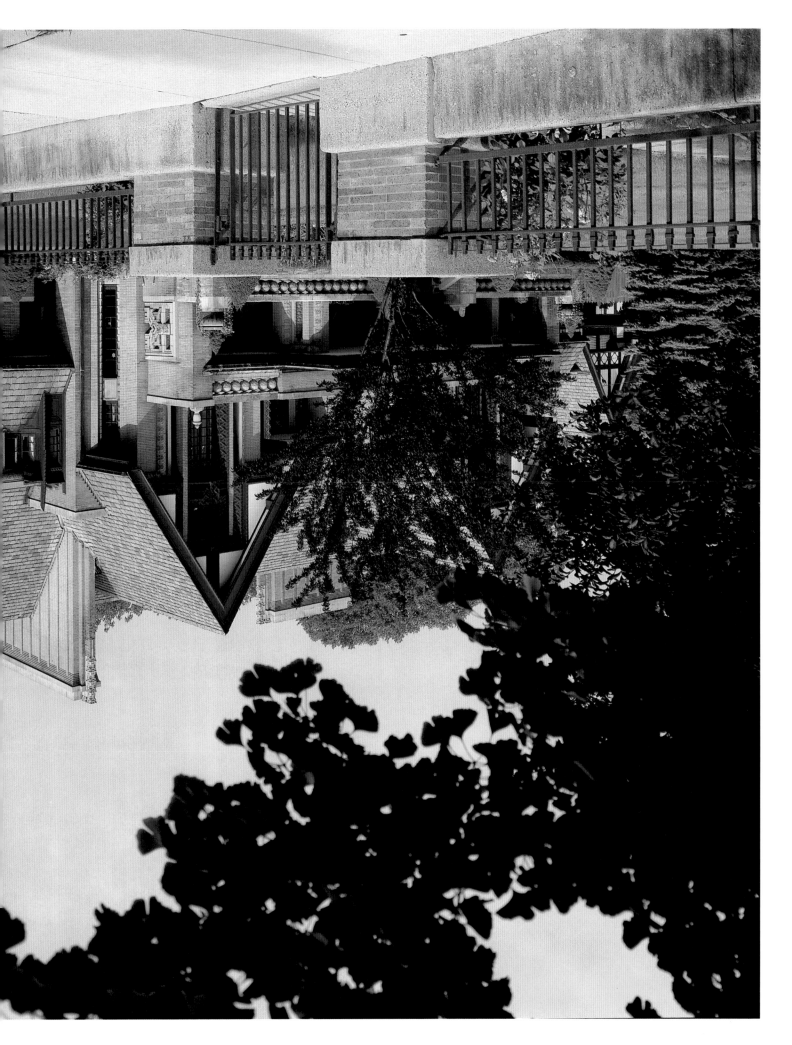

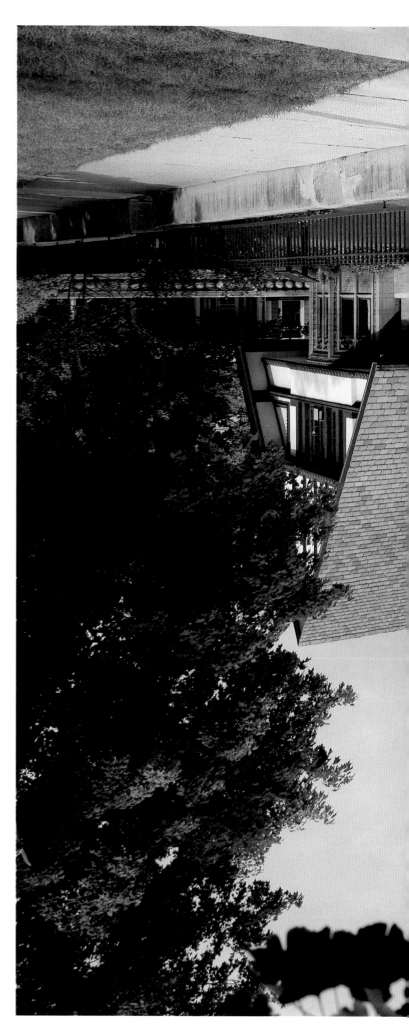

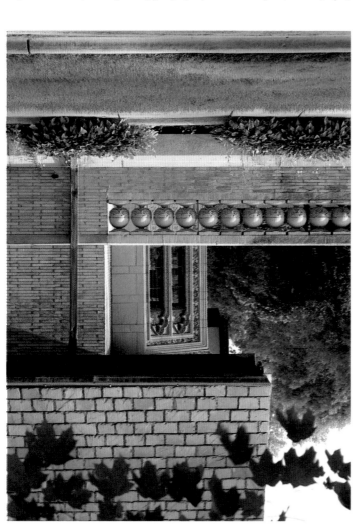

Left: A mansion by any standard, the Moore house is a case study in Wright's ability to draw upon many sources and synthesize them into something that was uniquely his own. Additionally, the remodeling necessitated by the fire of 1922 was an opportunity to improve upon the original design of almost 30 years earlier. This process of refinement and evolution was especially apparent in Wright's several home/studios, from the one in Oak Park to Taliesin in Spring Green, Wisconsin, and Taliesin West in Scottsdale, Arizona.

Above: Detail of the stone balustrade and a corner window of the Gothic type widely used in Tudor Revival architecture, which derived primarily from English Renaissance buildings of the 16th and early 17th centuries.

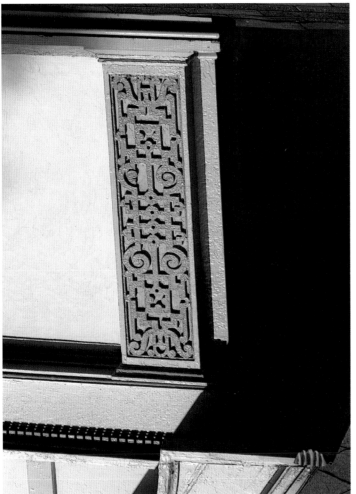

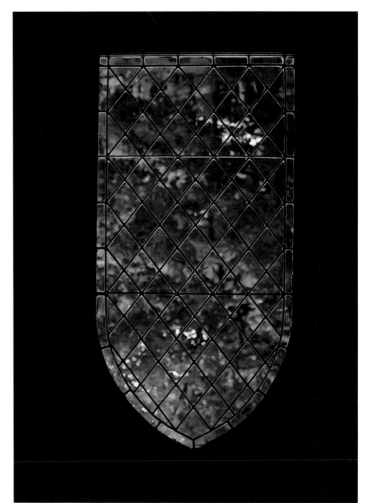

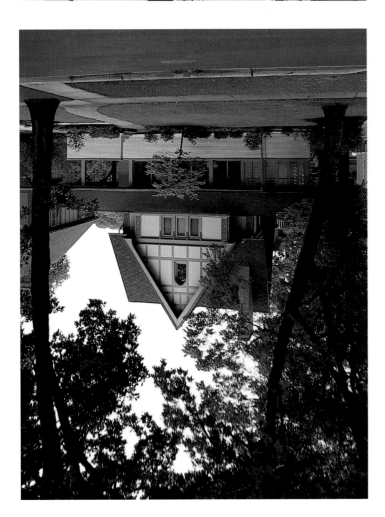

Harrison P. Young House, 1895

334 North Kenilworth Avenue

Right: A view of the Harrison P. Young house from the street shows the narrow-clapboard porch that runs the width of the house, built on the original foundations when Wright undertook this extensive remodeling commission in which the original structure was moved back 16 feet. The imitation half-timbering on the stuccoed gable is a later addition.

Bottom left: The diamond-paned Gothic-style window in the gable, a feature often found in Victorian houses, reflects the 19th-century interest in the picturesque as opposed to the classical in residential architecture.

Bottom right: A decorative panel in the naturalistic style of the Golden Door – the great portal created by Louis Sullivan for the Transportation Building at the World's Columbian Exposition in Chicago in 1893. Wright worked with Sullivan on the project.

Opposite: An octagonal bay lights the reception room, screened by Tuscan columns and spindles. The open floor plan introduced by Wright flows naturally into the living room, where the fireplace of Roman glazed brick and oak is visible.

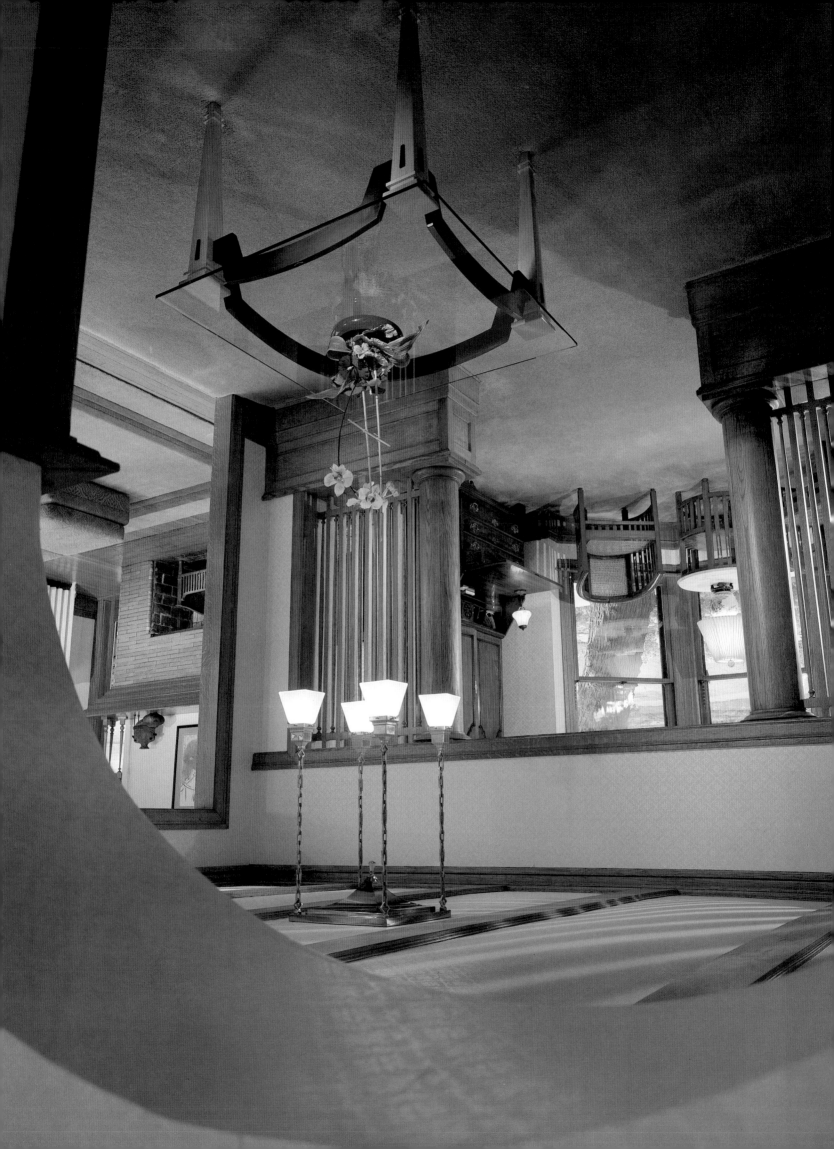

Harry C. Goodrich House, 1896
534 North East Avenue

George W. Furbeck House, 1897
223 North Euclid Avenue

Above: According to Storrer, the Goodrich house may have been based on a design originally offered to Charles Roberts. It has several features that portend later works, including location of the second-story windows, linked horizontally by the clapboards, directly below the eaves. The lower story includes a basement that is partially above ground, and the entry porch has been enclosed. The awnings are an addition Wright would have deplored; even screens offended him. Sometimes his aesthetic sense precluded comfort.

Above right: The soaring octagonal towers on each side of the entry to the George W. Furbeck house are an arresting feature and provide light to the rooms and stairwell they enclose.

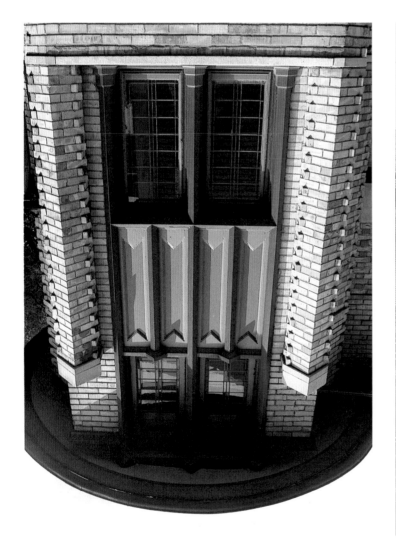

Opposite top: The original front porch of the George Furbeck house has been enlarged and enclosed, which alters the proportions. The brown brick and wood trim are as designed. The conical tower roofs contribute strength and interest to the structure.

Opposite bottom: The octagonal living room, with its string-courses, art-glass doors, and Roman brick fireplace, is characteristically warm and welcoming, with emphasis on the human scale rather than a sense of grandeur.

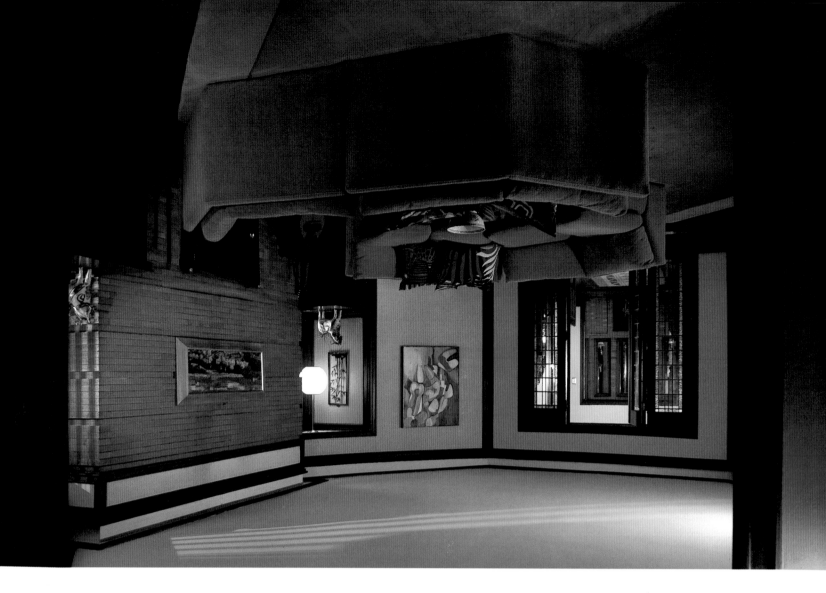

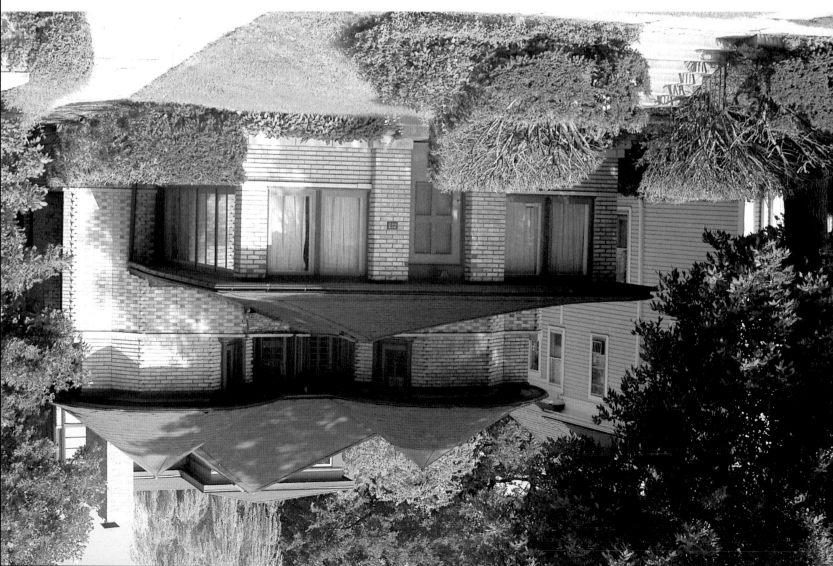

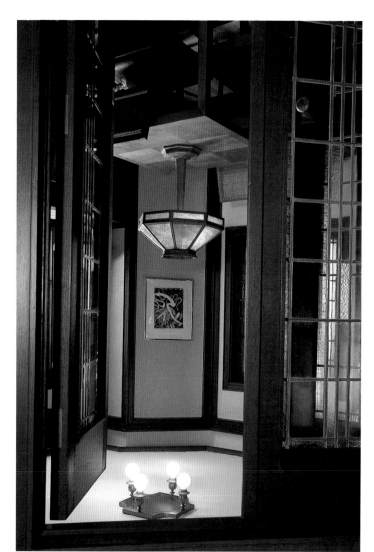

Left: The library in the south tower has a Wright-designed ceiling fixture and art-glass doors. The use of the octagon in this house is contemporary with Wright's incorporation of the form in the library at his own home studio. This was almost fifty years after Orson Fowler published his popular handbook *A Home for All,* which introduced plans for an eight-sided house designed to bring "comfortable dwellings within the reach of the poorer classes." (The octagonal plan could enclose some 20 percent more floor space within a wall of the same perimeter as that of the traditional "box" house, which Wright, too, deplored).

Opposite: The spacious dining room of the George Furbeck house has a particularly handsome fireplace of Roman brick and oak with inset mirrored panels.

Above: The plan for the first floor of the George Furbeck house shows that it extends deep into the lot and is much larger than it might appear from the front. The 17-foot-deep dining room adjoins the living room, with kitchen and utility areas at the back of the house. *The Frank Lloyd Wright Archives,* © *The Frank Lloyd Wright Foundation.*

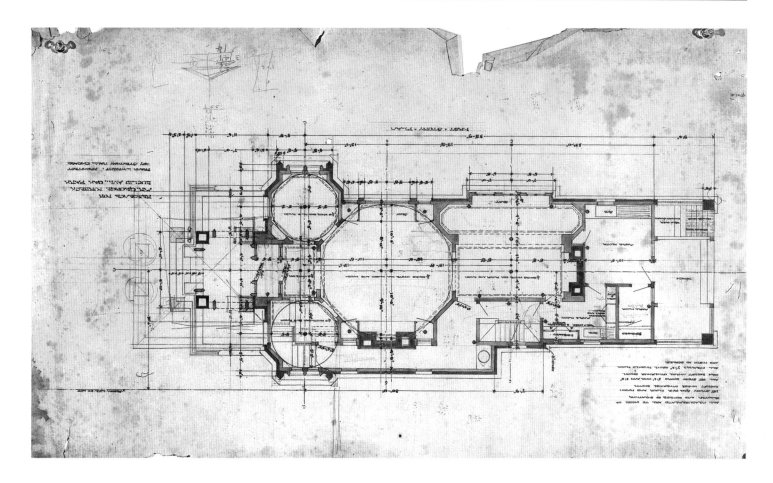

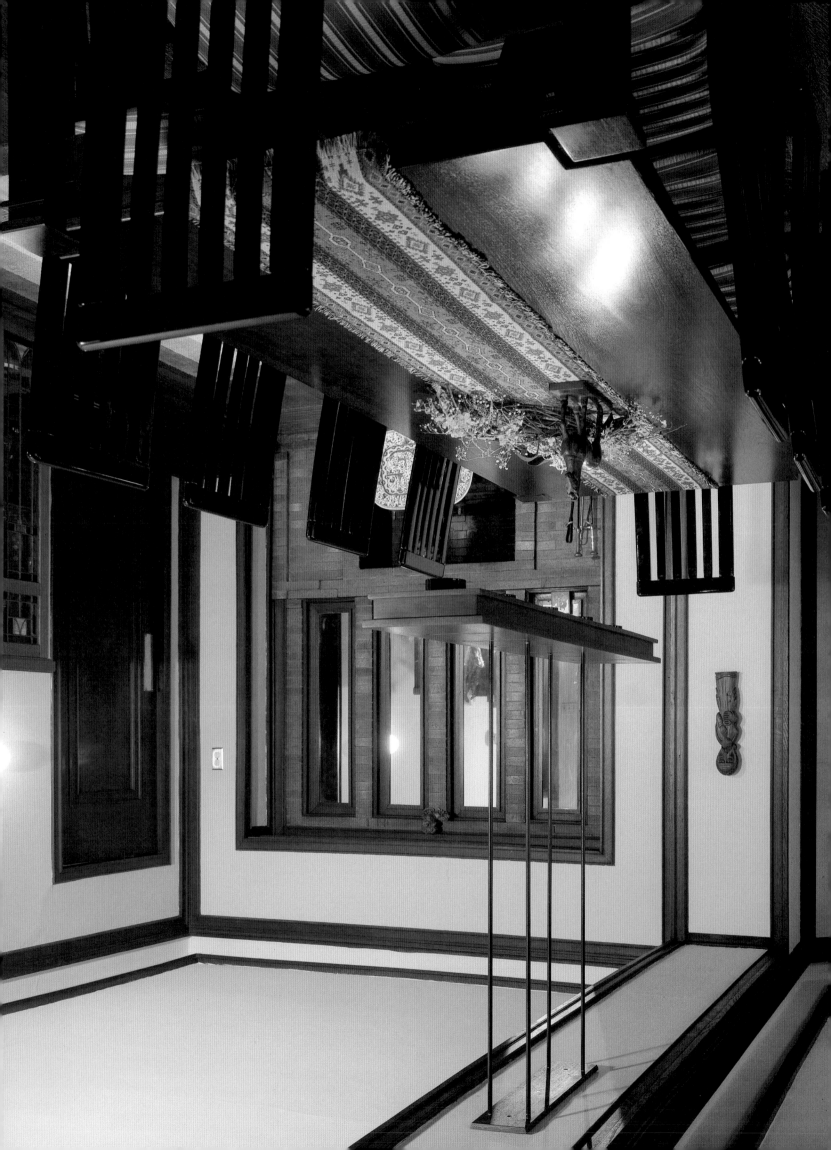

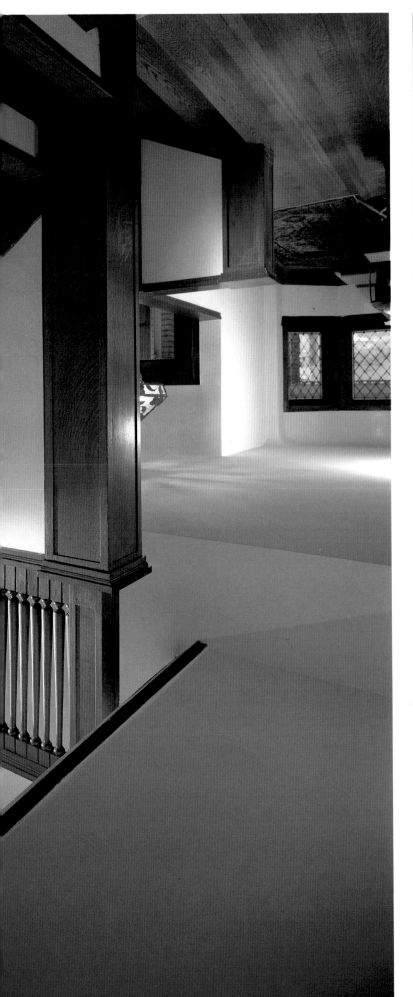

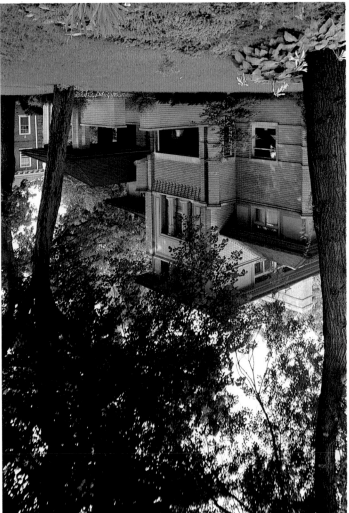

Rollin Furbeck House, 1897

511 North Fair Oaks Avenue

Below: Designed at the behest of Warren Furbeck for his son Rollin, this three-story residence is notable for its imposing facade incorporating decorative plaster columns, brick, and painted wood trim. The broad eaves of the hipped roof unite with the symmetrical upper-story windows in a band of stucco.

Right: Movement toward the Prairie house is apparent in the flowing interior space of the Rollin Furbeck house, based on a cruciform plan. The wide stairwell alternates light risers with dark treads and molding, while the balustrade gives a vertical thrust.

Far right: At the second level, recessed diamond-paned casement windows are fronted by plaster columns above the light tan brick of the ground-floor facade.

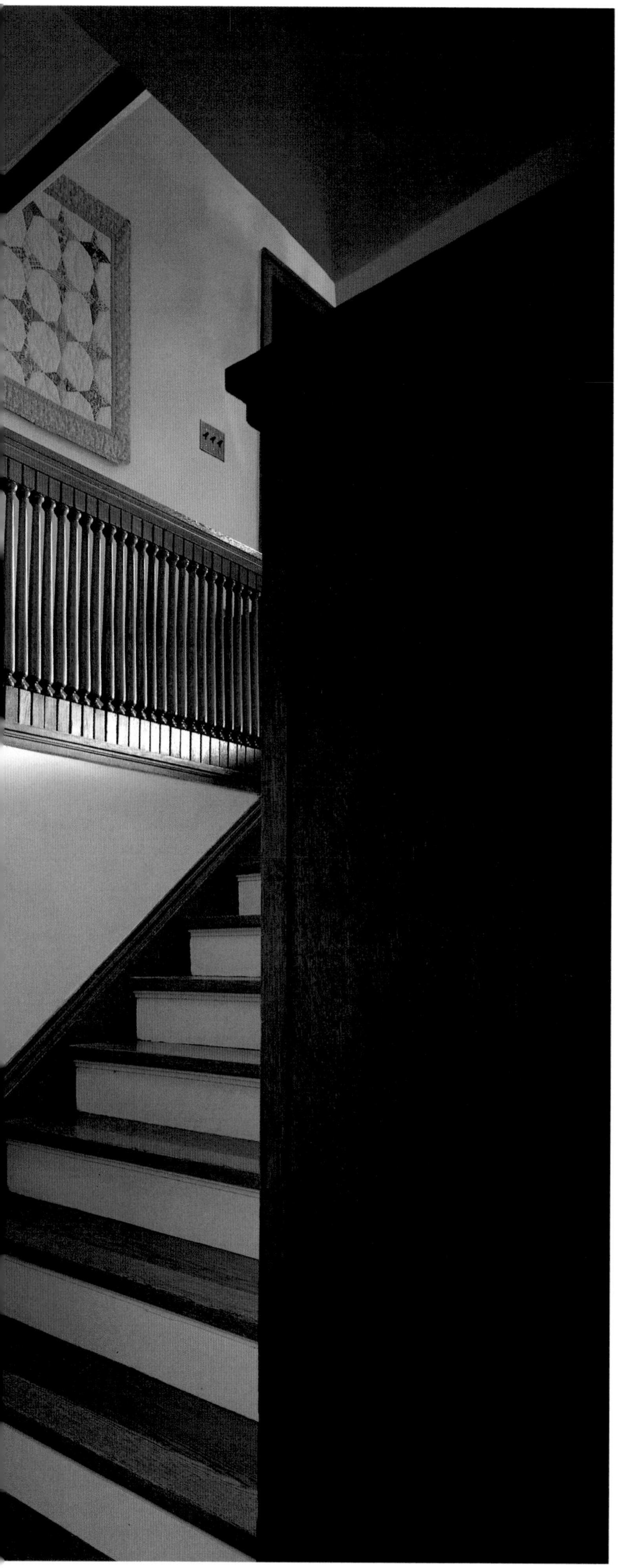

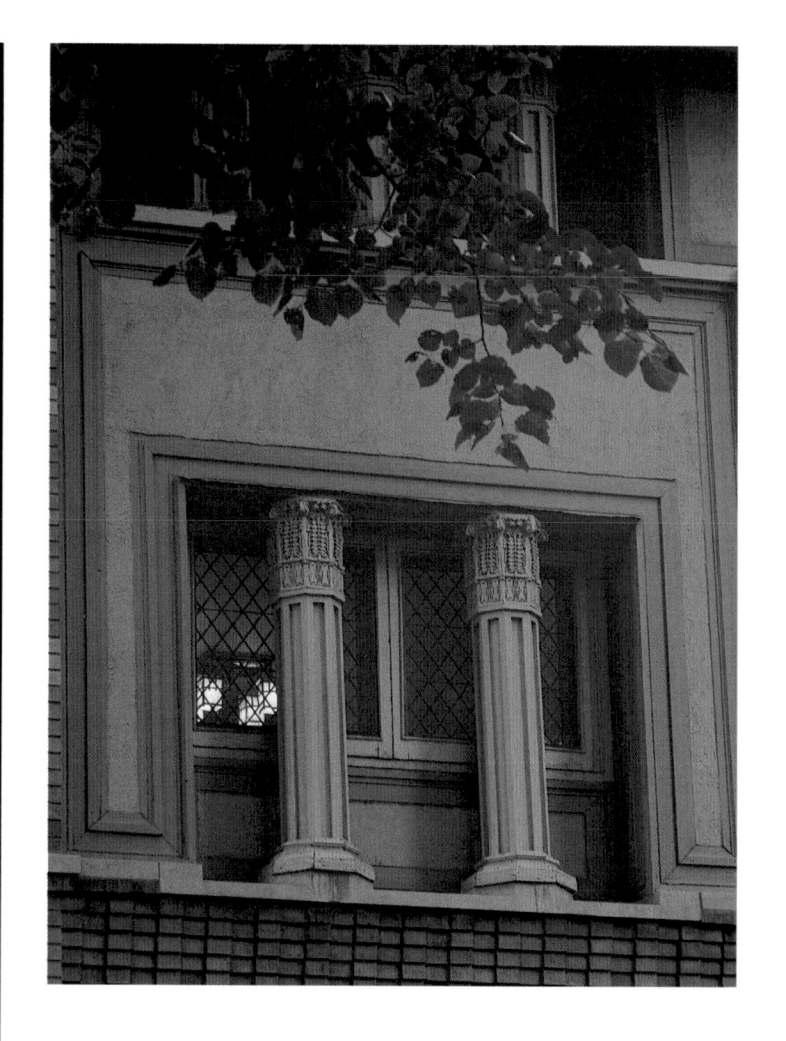

George W. Smith House, 1898
404 South Home Avenue

Below: No plans are available for the Smith house which has been considerably altered since 1898. Notable features include the massive rectangular chimneys and the multilevel steeply pitched roof with flaring eaves that suggest Japanese influence. *Photo by Hedrich Blessing.*

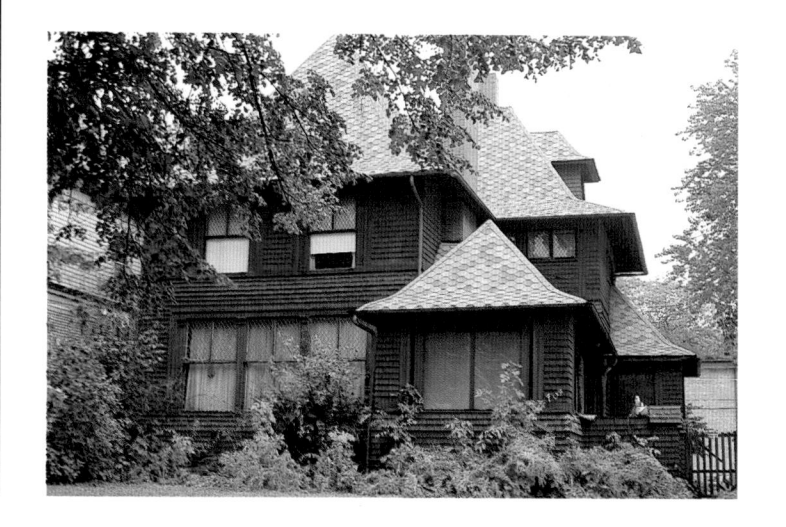

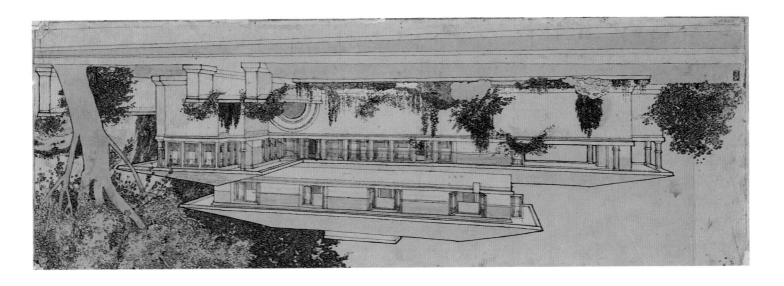

Frank W. Thomas House, 1901

210 North Forest Avenue

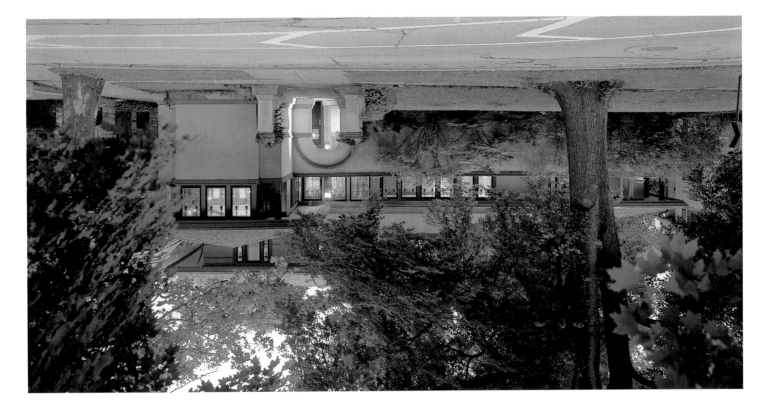

Above: The Frank W. Thomas house was Wright's first Prairie house in Oak Park. Laid out on an L-shaped plan, it has no excavated basement. The arched entryway is screened by walls, and the structure is self-contained, yielding a strong sense of privacy and enclosure. The main living space is above ground level, lighted by bands of casement windows.

Below: Perspective of the imposing Thomas house, with its long terrace and covered porch. *The Frank Lloyd Wright Archives,* © *The Frank Lloyd Wright Foundation.*

Opposite: Exceptional art glass of Wright's design and recessed lighting are notable features of the Thomas house.

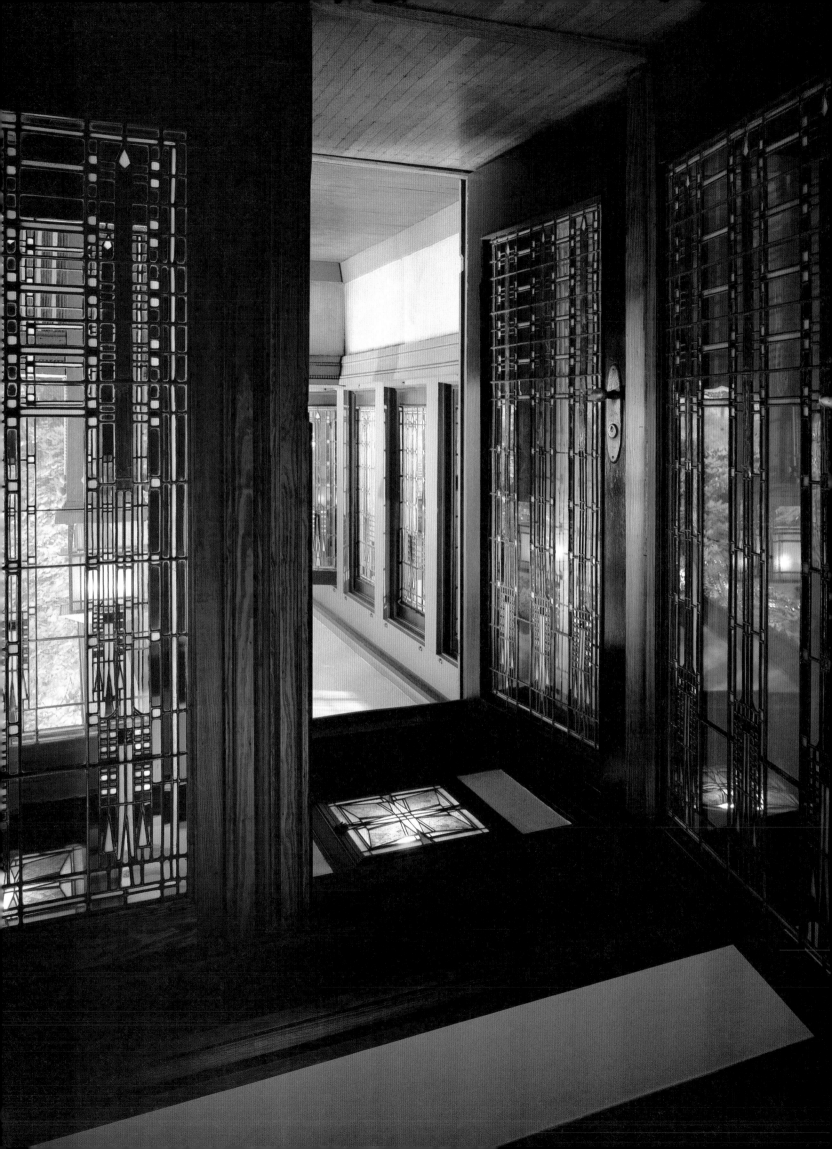

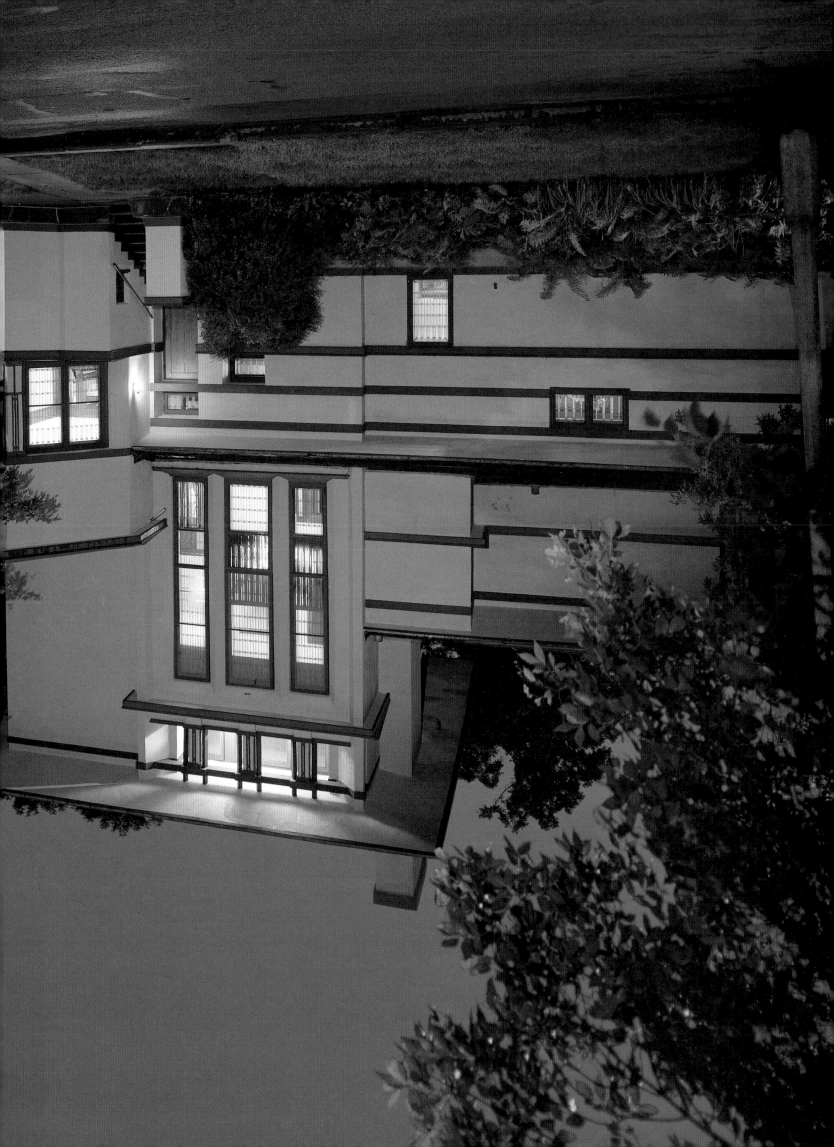

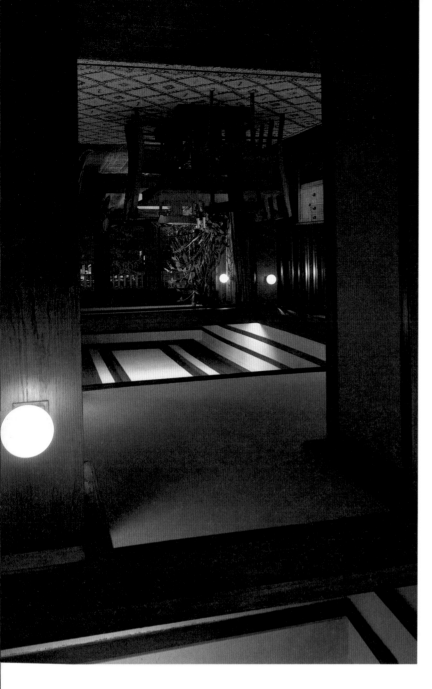

William G. Fricke House, 1901
540 North Fair Oaks Avenue

Left: The stately Fricke house shows Secessionist influence in its three-story ascent to the band of windows that meet the soffit and in the massing of various geometric forms. Fenestration varies from the small clerestory windows on the left to the two-story expanse at the main level. Webster Tomlinson collaborated on the design.

Below: The richly paneled space of the dining room is defined by the ceiling treatment, a forerunner of that used for the landmark Robie house in Chicago (1906).

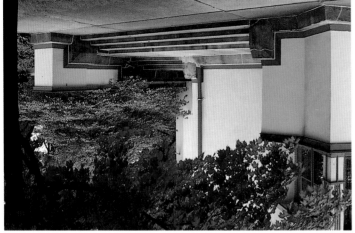

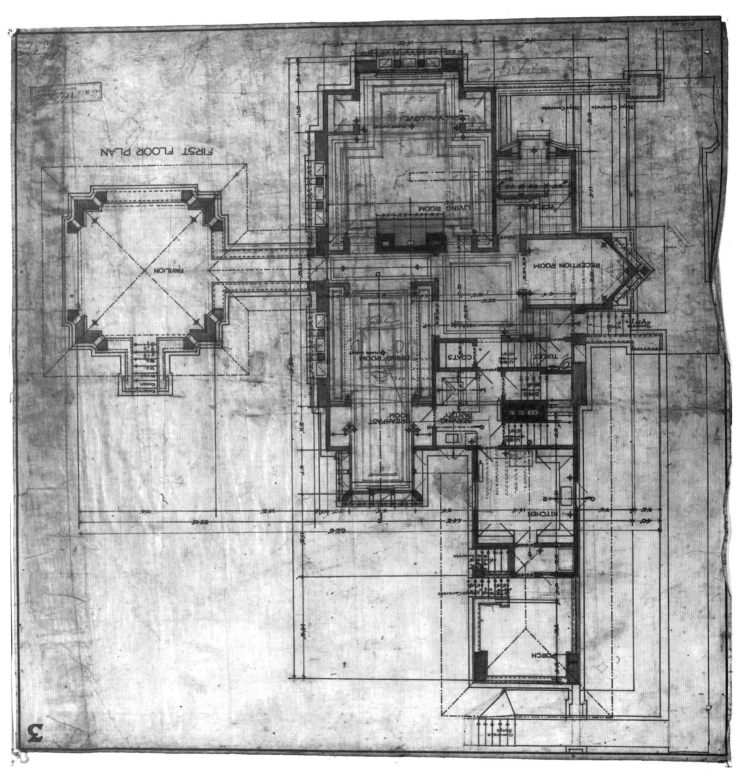

Above: The first-floor plan of the Fricke house shows the central hall, reception-room bay, and large living and dining rooms. A breakfast room adjoins the pantry and kitchen. The semi-detached pavillion has since been demolished. *The Frank Lloyd Wright Archives, © The Frank Lloyd Wright Foundation.*

Right: The shallow stone steps leading to the off-center entryway to the Fricke house.

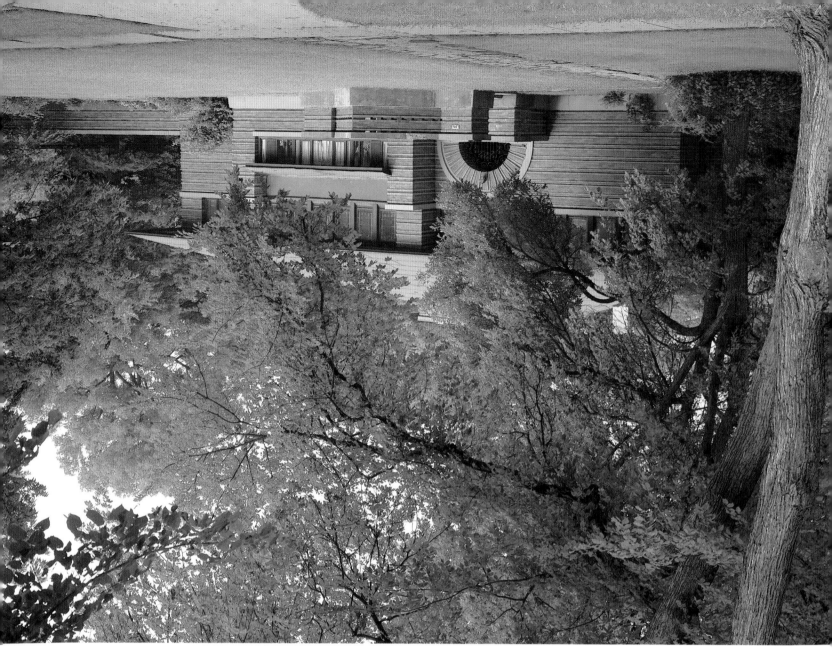

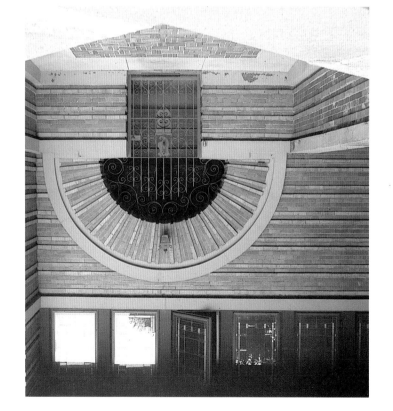

Arthur Heurtley House, 1902

318 North Forest Avenue

Right: The Arthur Heurtley house is faced with Roman brick laid in courses that suggest board and batten. The arched entryway is partially concealed by brick walls and opens into living quarters above ground level.

Below: The four-square Heurtley house, with its low hipped roof, was designed for clients who took great pleasure in entertaining; the main living area, with breakfast alcove, comprises more than a thousand square feet. The house is only half a block from the Wright home and residence.

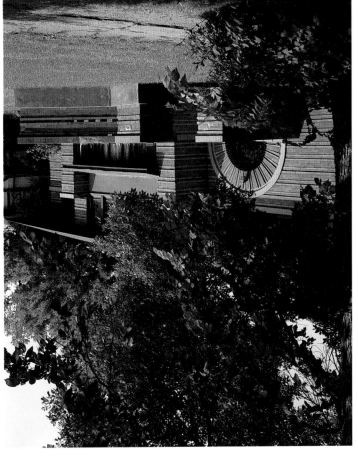

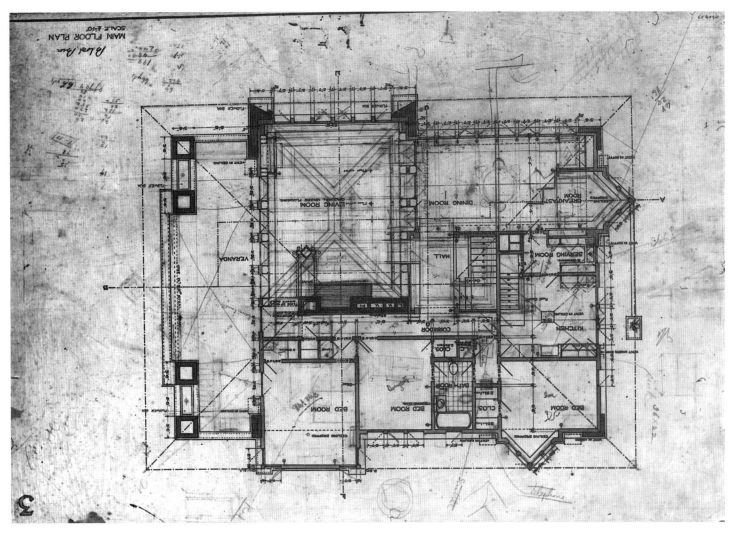

Above: Main-floor plan for the Heurtley house, showing the fifty-two-foot-long veranda that has since been enclosed. The bedrooms were grouped at the rear along a central corridor. The breakfast room alcove is an extension of the long, rectangular dining room. *The Frank Lloyd Wright Archives, © The Frank Lloyd Wright Foundation.*

Right: The stylobate foundation below the low brick piers is typical of the Prairie house, which is not dissimilar to a Tuscan or Umbrian villa in its horizontal profile.

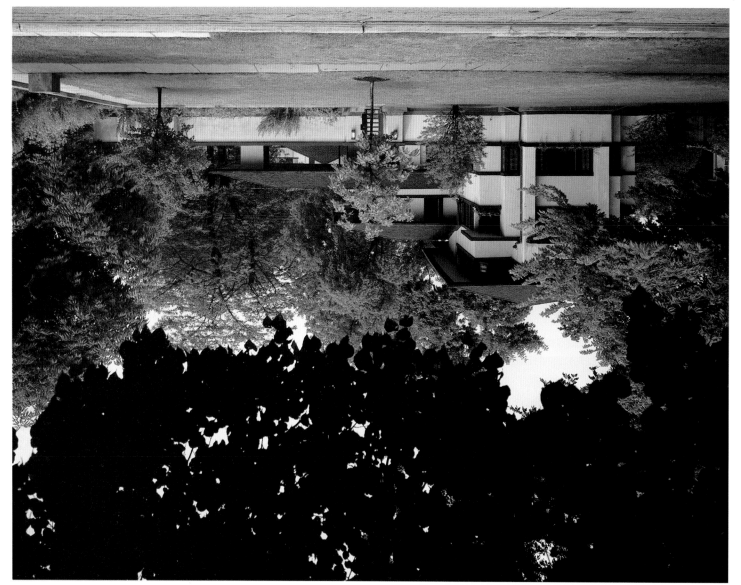

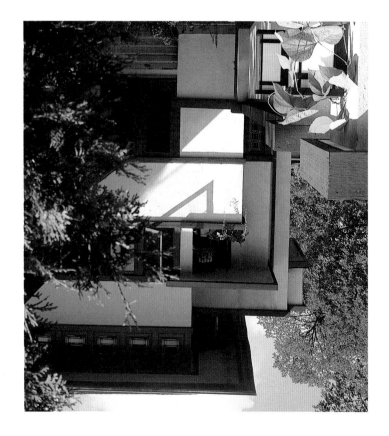

William E. Martin House, 1903

636 North East Avenue

Right: In the house built for William E. Martin, the horizontal is emphasized by long wings on the ground floor and by the extension of both trim and windows around corners.

Below: Multilevel hipped roofs give the Martin house a graceful ascent from street level to top story. The front entry opens both to the hall and to the long veranda, which unites the house and its spacious grounds.

Above: Art-glass screen panels and skylights enhance the warm ambience of the Martin house hallway, with its built-in sideboard and seating. Decorative features like the vase filled with golden-rod are in keeping with Wright's aesthetic, which favored the use of native plants.

Opposite: The living room of the Martin house, in which the client gave Wright a free hand with respect to design of furniture and fittings. Martin was entirely satisfied with the results and pro-vided valuable recommendations to other clients, including his brother Darwin D. Martin, for whom Wright built a Prairie-style mansion in Buffalo, New York.

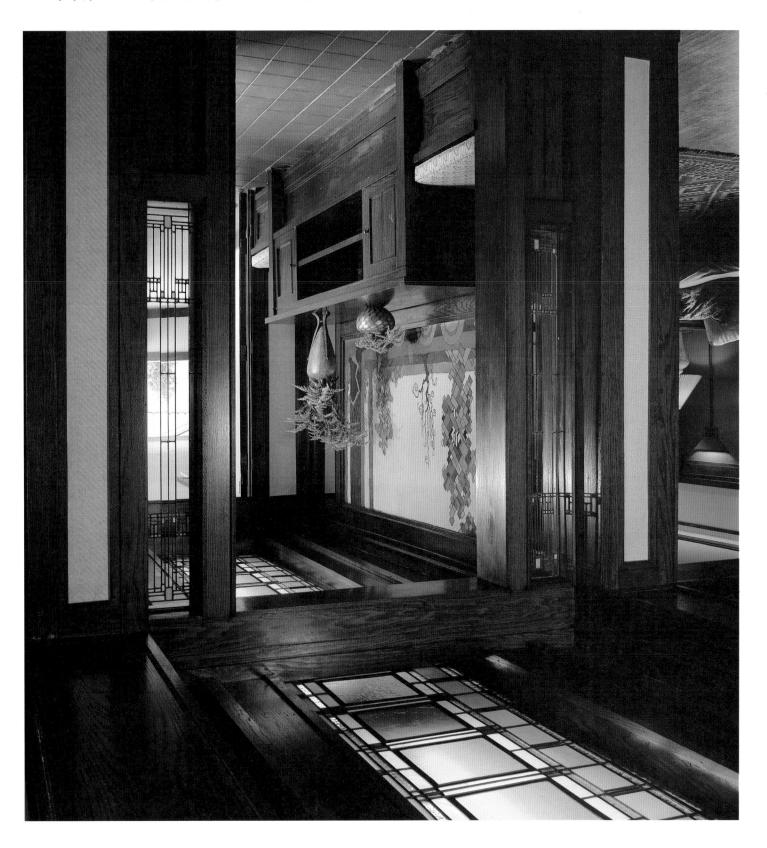

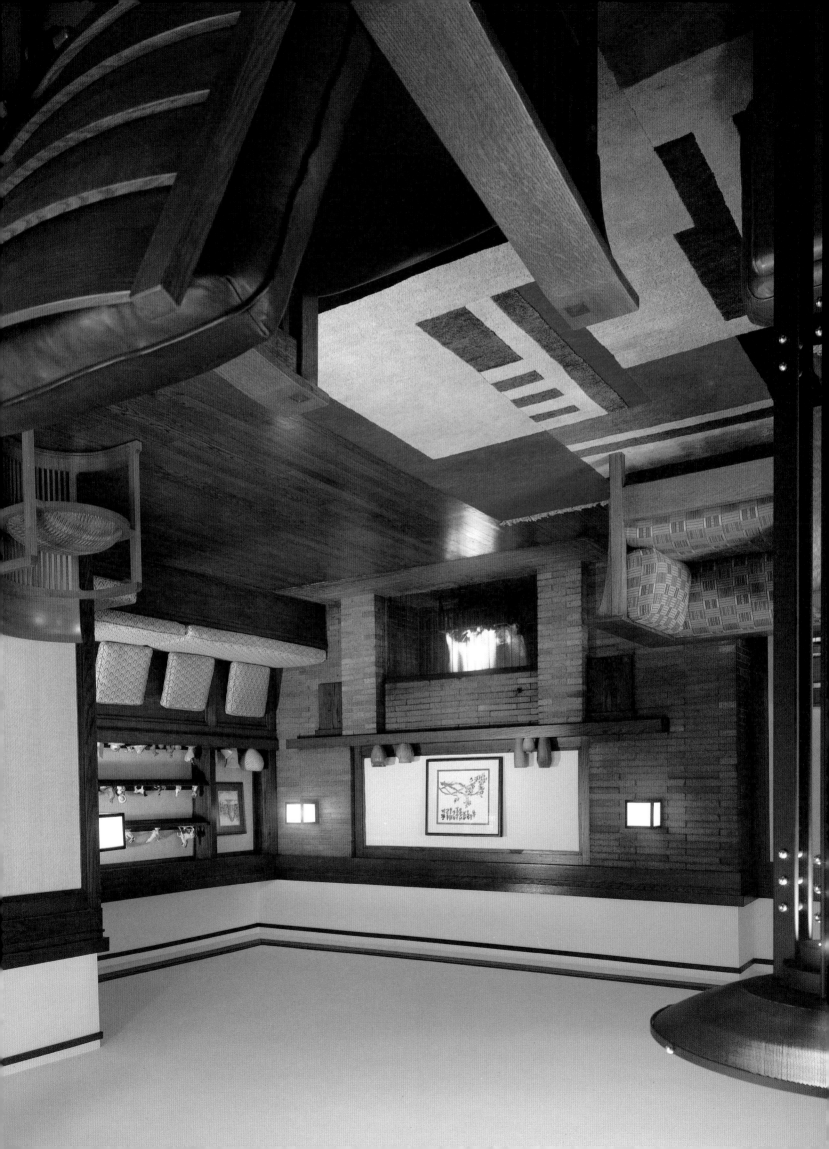

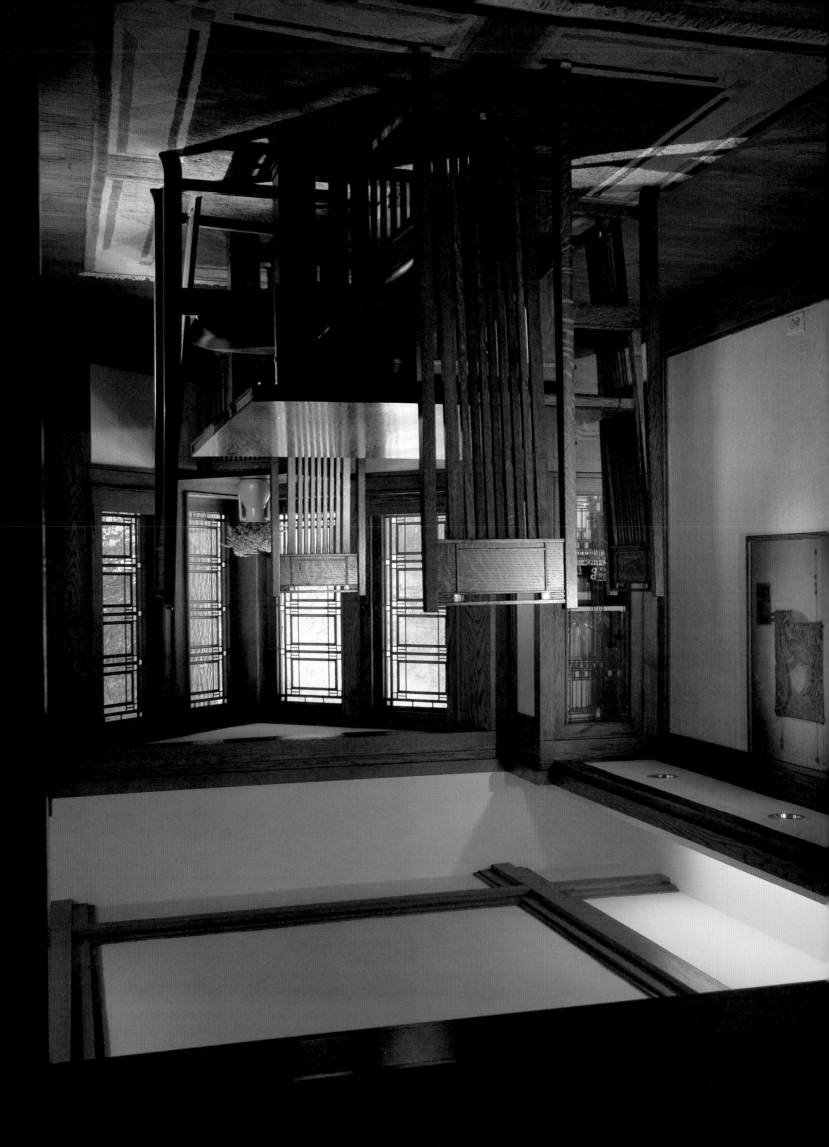

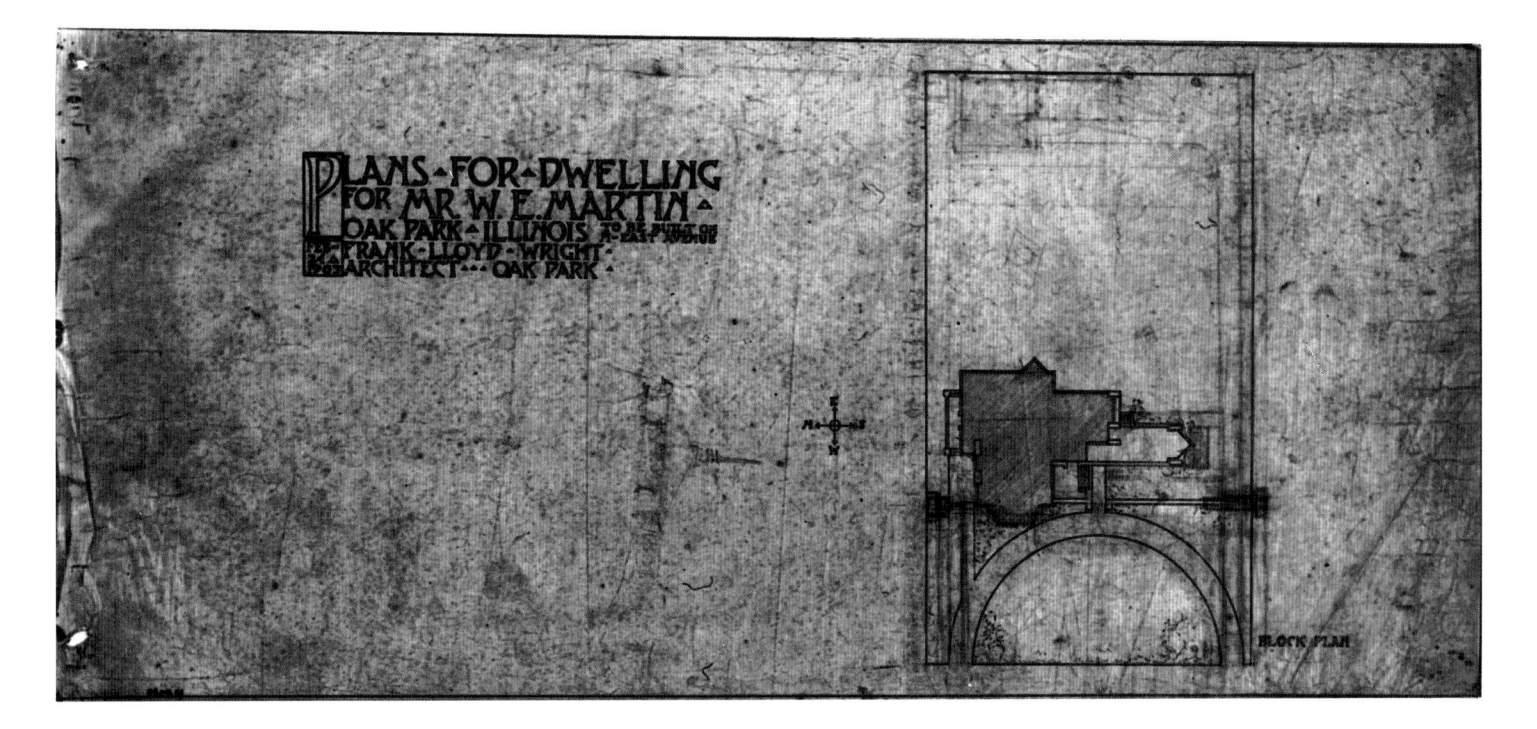

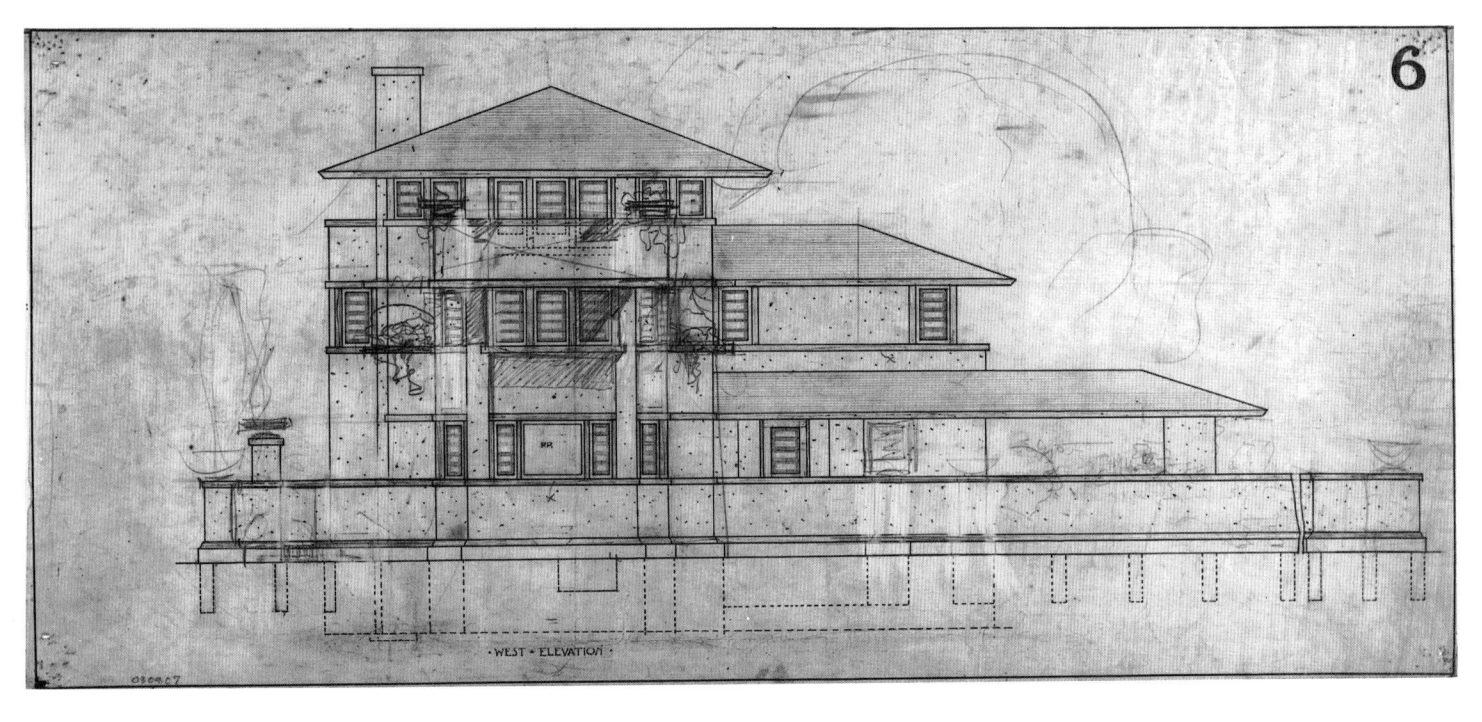

Opposite: Multiplane bay windows with lead cames illuminate the Martin house dining room, which has a built-in china closet with art-glass front. The high-backed oak chairs around the table contribute to the sense of enclosure in the dining area.

Above top: Block plan for the Martin house, which faces North East Avenue. *The Frank Lloyd Wright Archives,* © *The Frank Lloyd Wright Foundation.*

Above: West elevation of the Martin house, which was meticulously landscaped by Wright's colleagues Walter Burley Griffin. In 1909 it overlooked a pergola joined to one of the porches, as well as gardens, pools, and a lawn tennis court. *The Frank Lloyd Wright Archives,* © *The Frank Lloyd Wright Foundation.*

Edwin H. Cheney House, 1904
520 North East Avenue

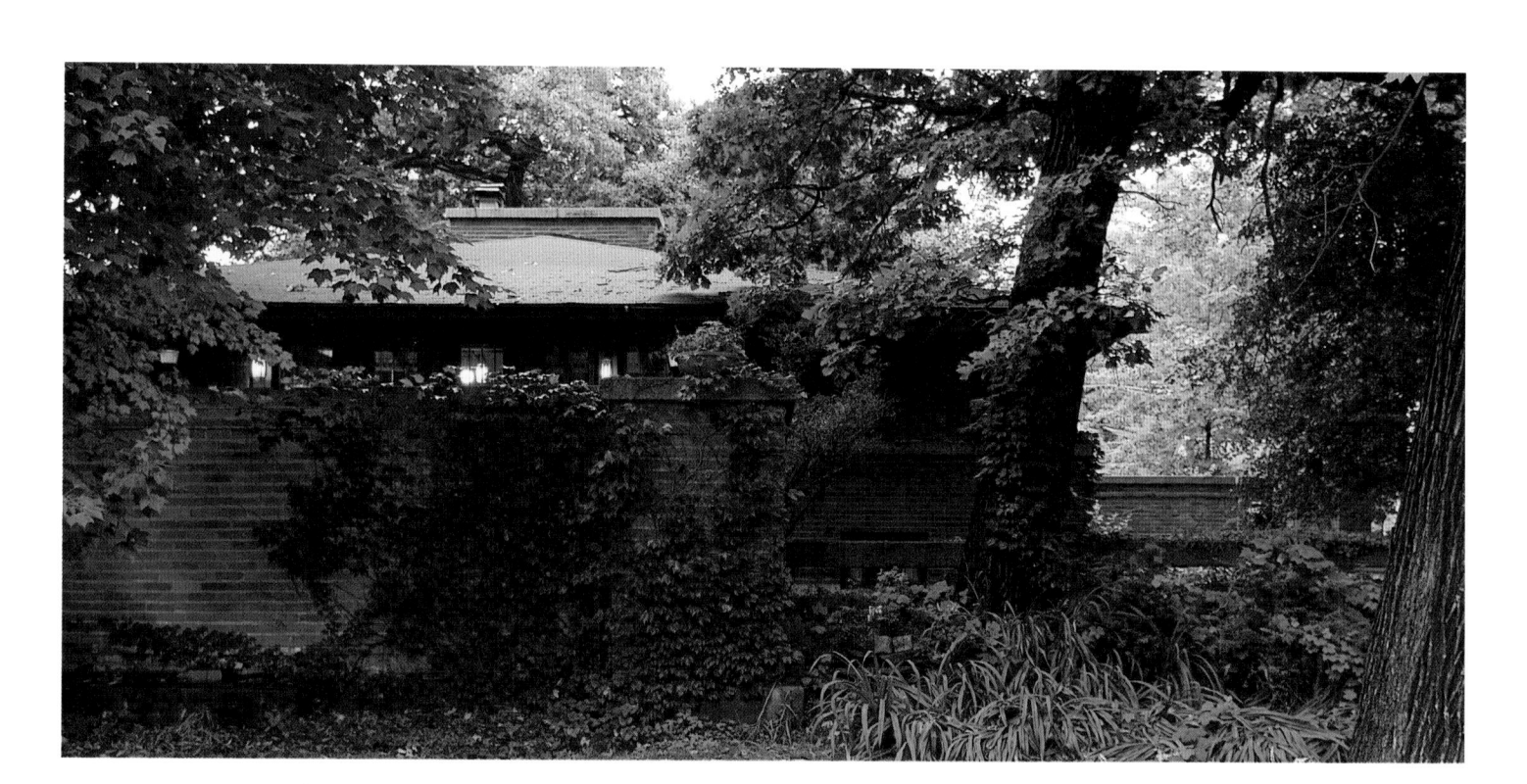

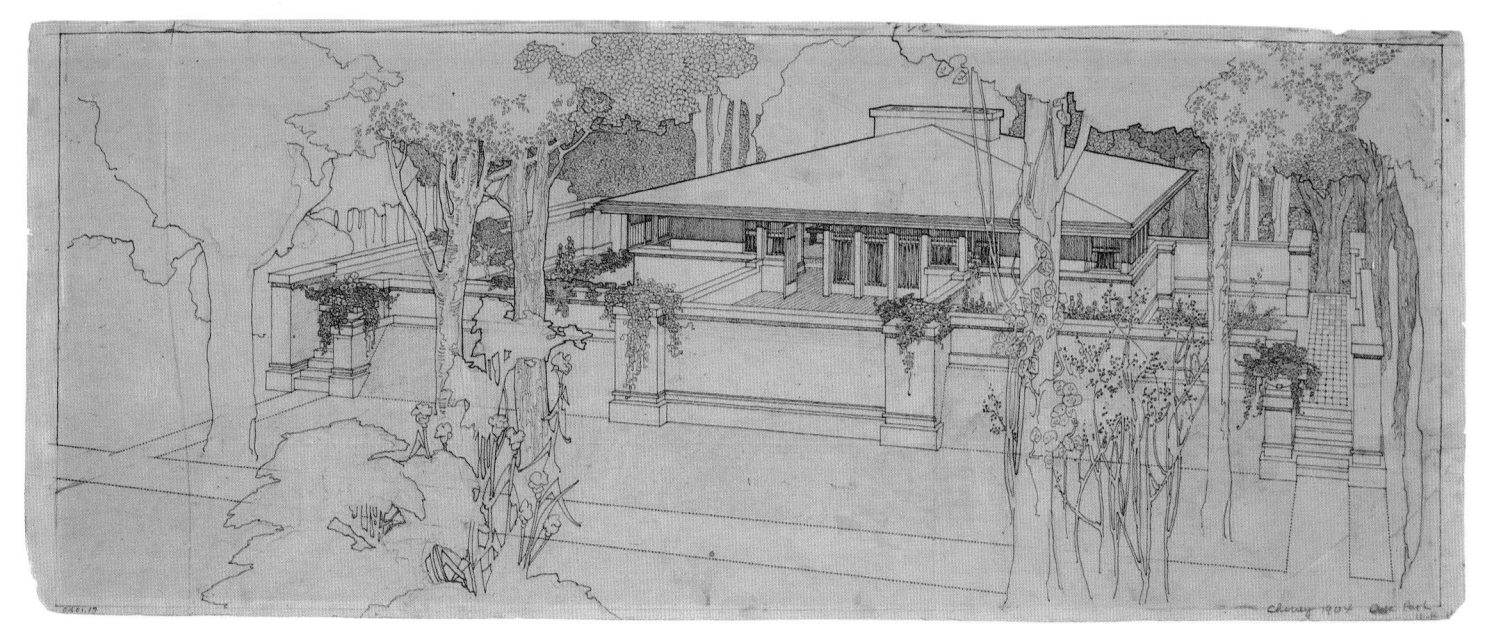

Above top: Another Wright residence on North East Avenue is the secluded single-story Cheney house, with a high brick wall enclosing its terrace. There is, in fact, a "basement," at the lower level, which has windows with sills at ground level.

Above: Perspective of the Cheney house and grounds. *The Frank Lloyd Wright Archives,* © *The Frank Lloyd Wright Foundation.*

Opposite: Wright's signature is clear in the living room of the Cheney house, with its built-in bookcase, art-glass lamps and lighting fixtures, and ribbed vaulted ceiling. The house has fifty-two windows of iridescent art glass.

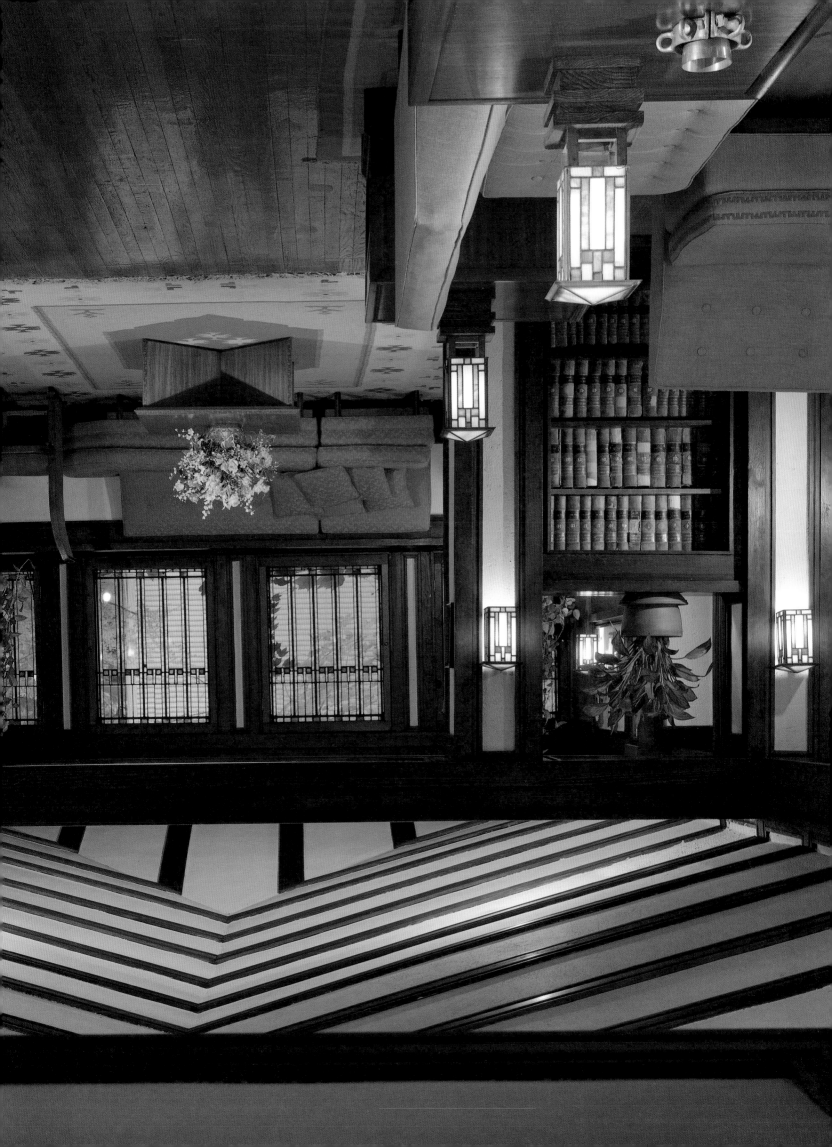

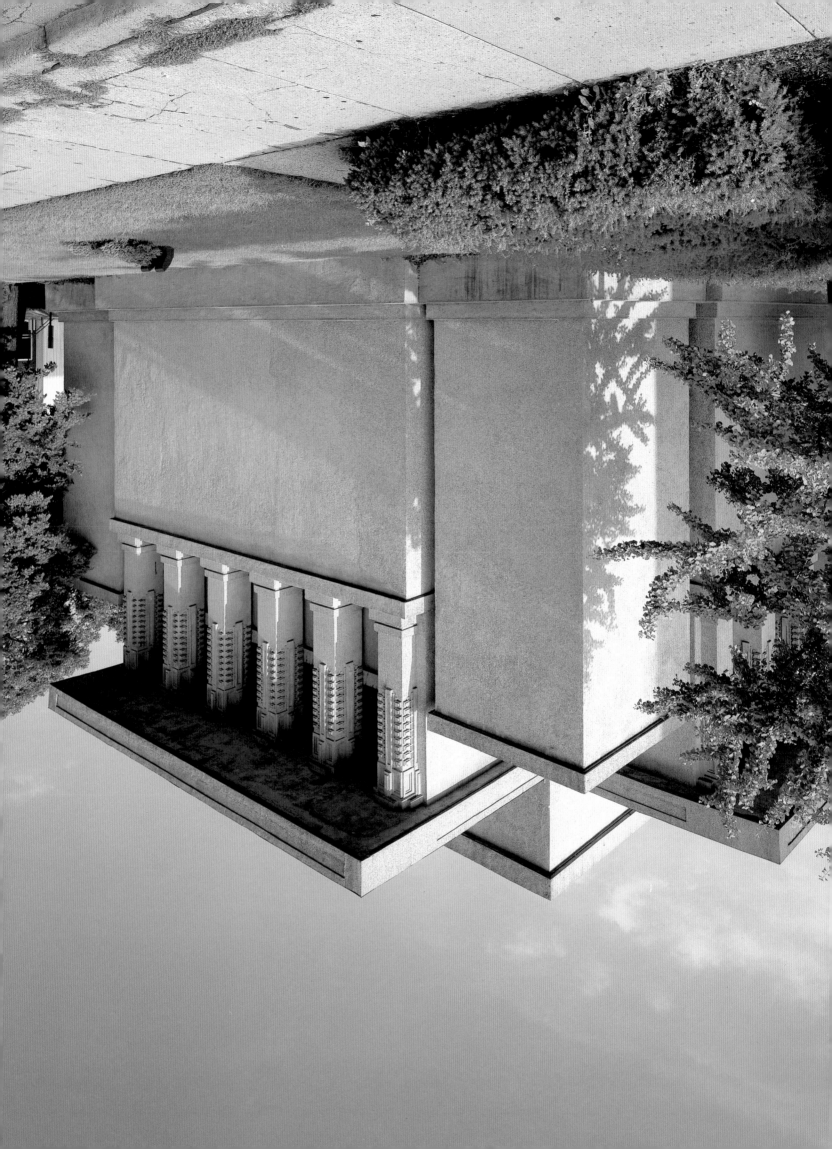

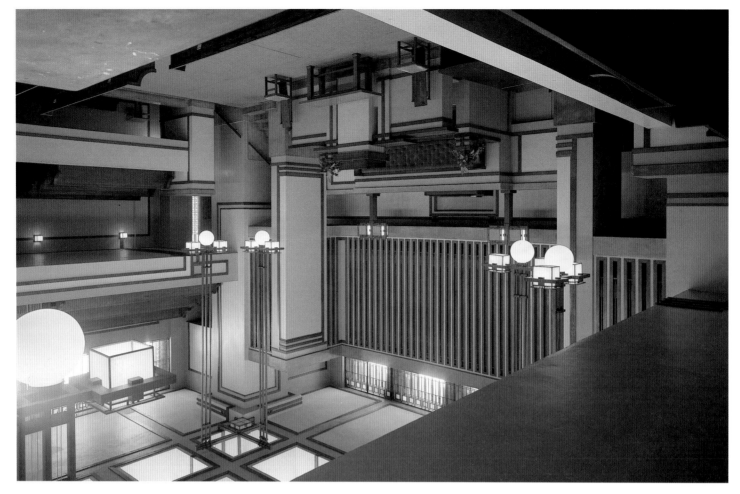

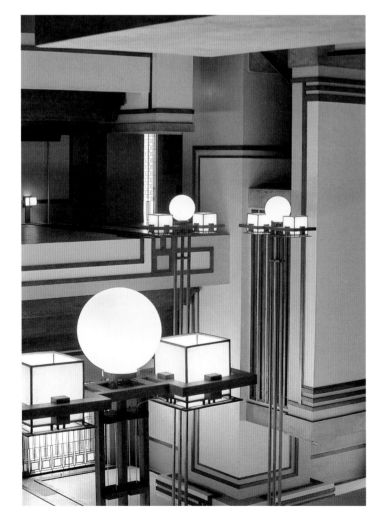

Unity Temple, 1904
875 West Lake Street

Opposite: The poured concrete with an exposed pebble exterior surface makes Unity Temple a monolithic structure, symmetrical in form and largely opaque. Stairwells are housed in the pylons at the four corners of the building. Exterior ornamentation is limited to the squarish concrete columns along the façade, which have a Mayan look. The slab roof juts out at various levels.

Right: Horizontal and vertical moldings define the worship space, along with the lighting fixtures in which cubes and spheres alternate. These fixtures echo the plan of the building – a Greek cross in a square.

Below: Art-glass clerestory windows and skylights provide the natural light in the worship space of Unity Temple, which is an introverted enclosure with peripheral balconies served by the stairs within the pylons.

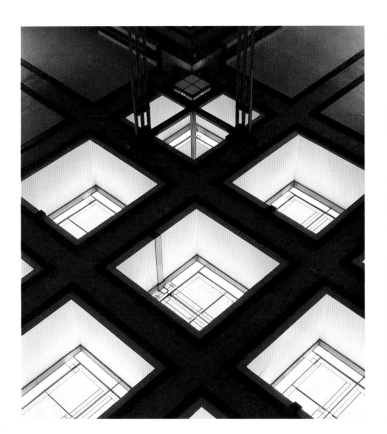

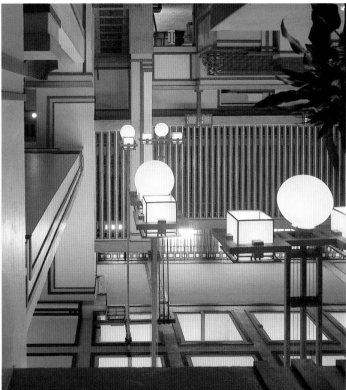

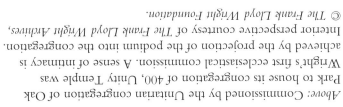

Above: Commissioned by the Unitarian congregation of Oak Park to house its congregation of 400, Unity Temple was Wright's first ecclesiastical commission. A sense of intimacy is achieved by the projection of the podium into the congregation. Interior perspective courtesy of *The Frank Lloyd Wright Archives,* © *The Frank Lloyd Wright Foundation.*

Bottom left: The simple elegance of Wright's interior gives a sense of concentration and presence that excludes the world outside.

Below: The skylights are deeply recessed in the ceiling grid, their square shapes reprising that of the building plan.

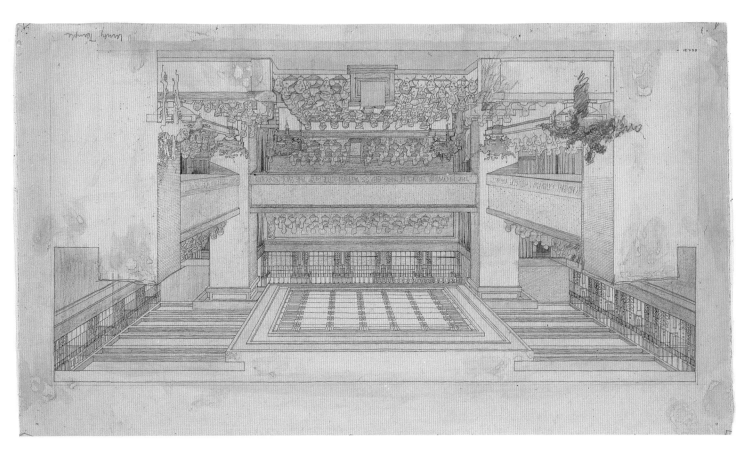

OAK PARK

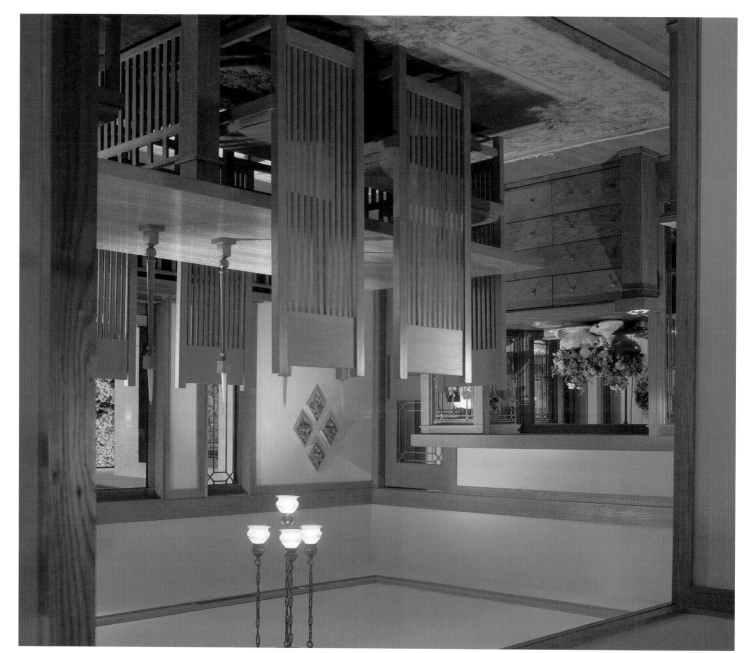

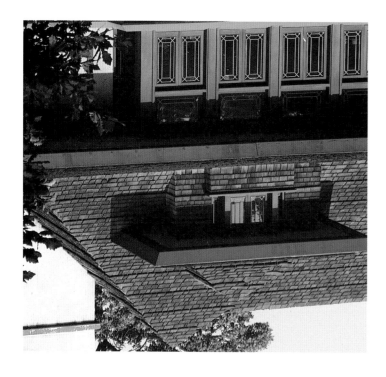

E.R. Hills-DeCaro House,
1906, 1976–77
313 North Forest Avenue

Right: The Prairie-style Hills-DeCaro house was remodeled from a Victorian house at the behest of Nathan Moore, who moved it to its present location in 1906. Casement windows and exterior banding of the stucco surface are characteristic of this period. On the roof, a double layer of shingles every fifth row emphasizes the horizontal.

Below: The dining room was impeccably restored by the DeCaros and architect John D. Tilton after the DeCaros purchased the house, in a state of disrepair, in 1975.

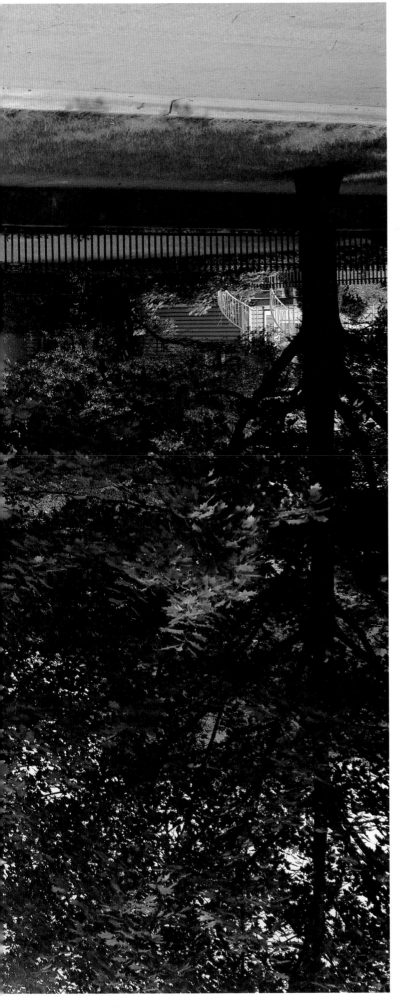

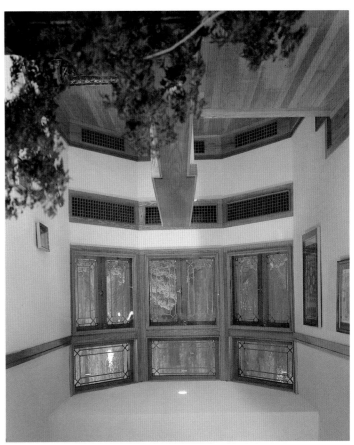

Above: The octagonal art-glass bay at the second-floor landing of the Hills-DeCaro house. Grillework conceals the radiators.

Right: As seen from Forest Avenue, the restored Hills-DeCaro house has an air of dignity and comfort. Its natural textures and horizontal profile, accented by broad, hovering roof planes, are in concert with the serene, tree-studded setting.

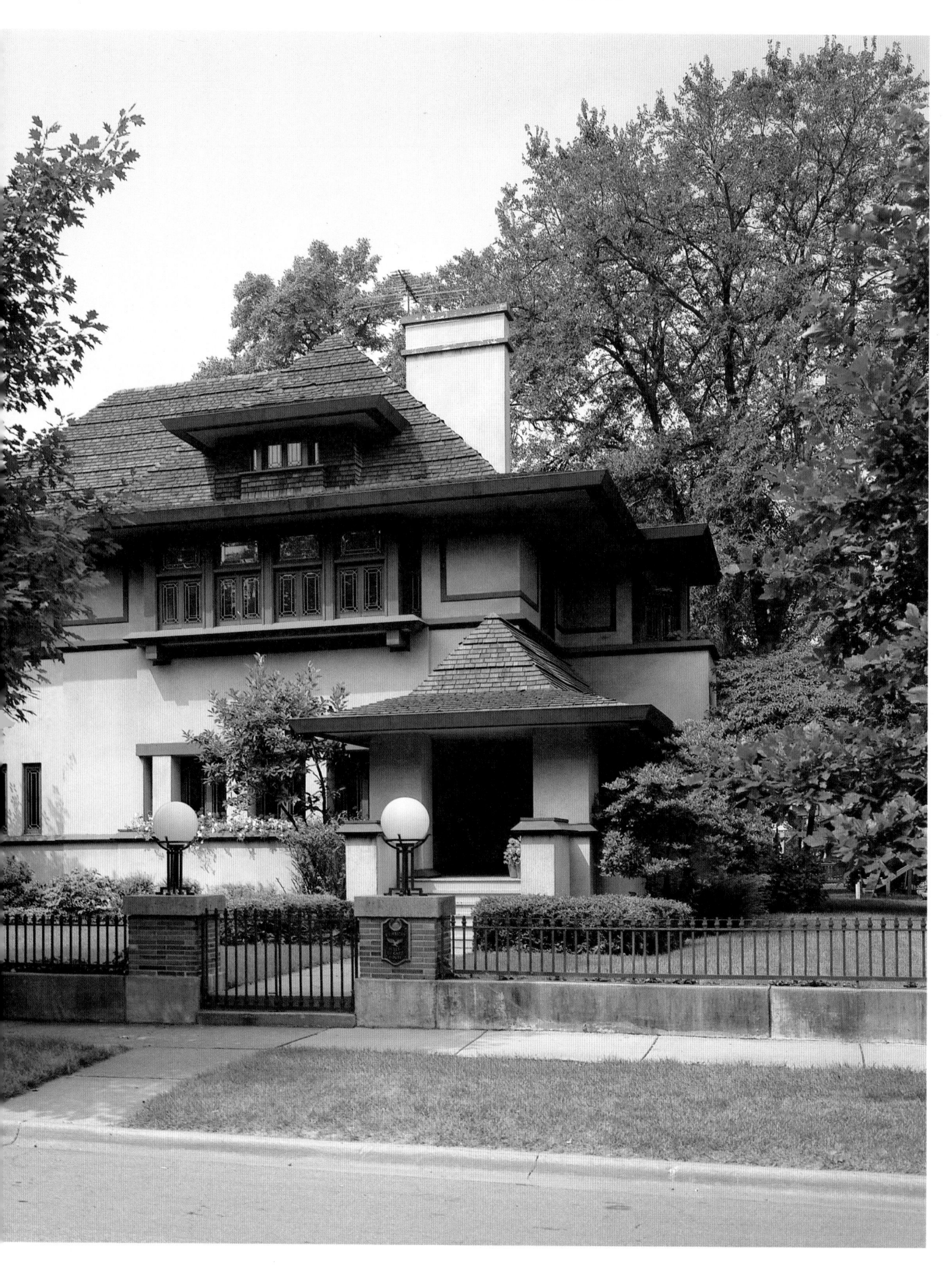

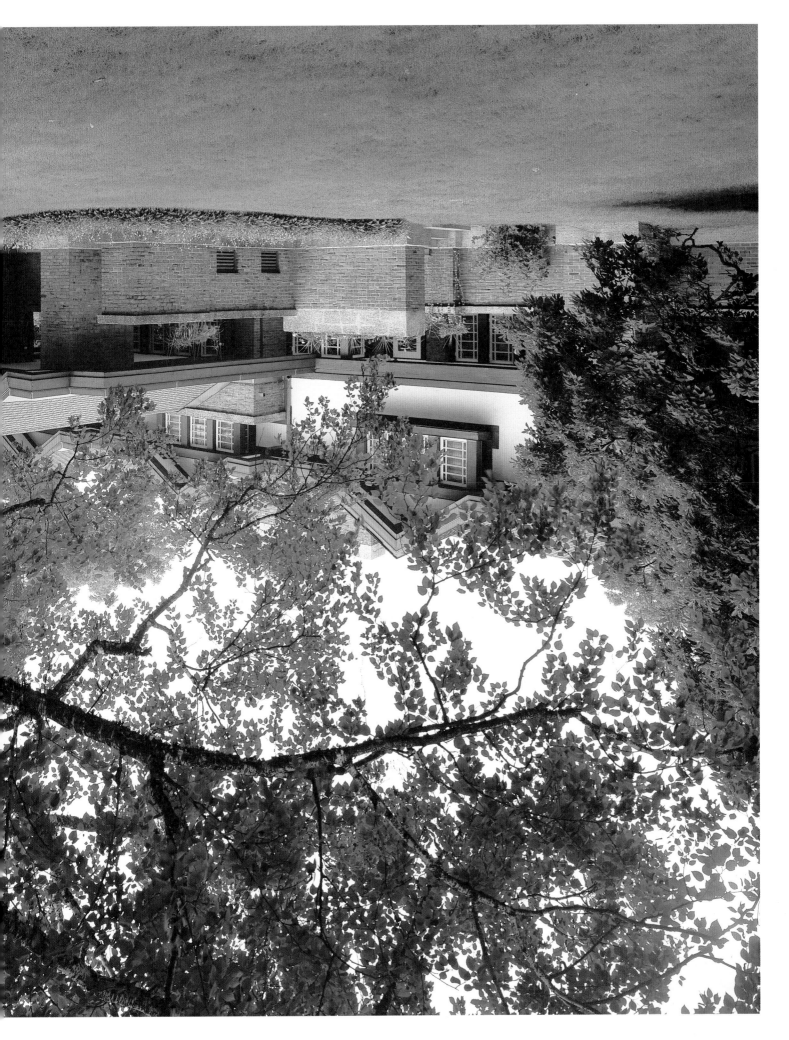

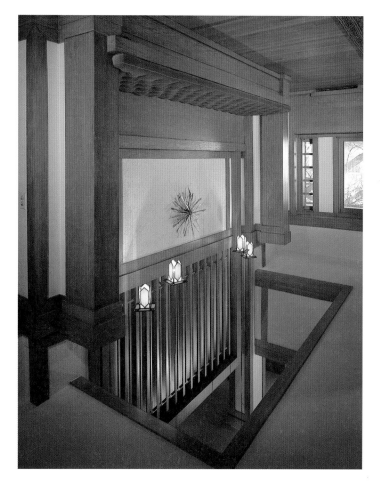

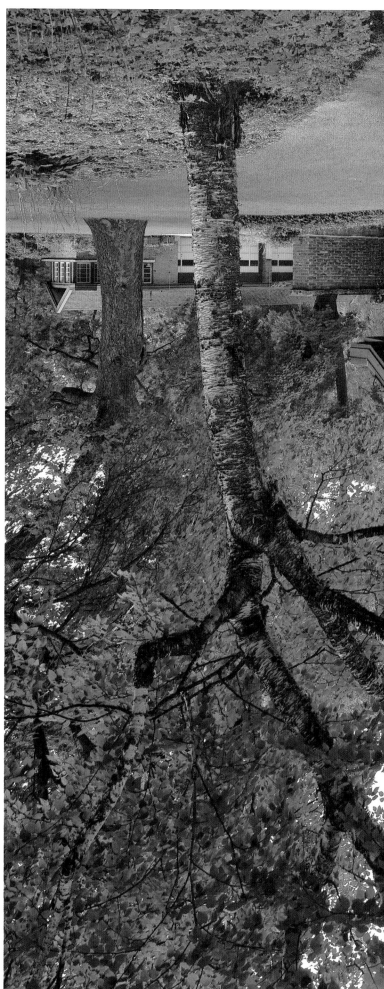

Peter A. Beachy House, 1906

238 North Forest Avenue

Left: The imposing Prairie house designed for Peter A. Beachy occupies a very large lot and was originally a Gothic-style cottage. Of brick and plaster, with wood trim, it has many elements typical of the large suburban house in this mode, including grouped casements, buttress piers, a concealed entryway on the north wall, and broad bands of stonework.

Below: The two-story hallway of the Beachy house has a long upholstered bench built in between wooden piers, with the wall behind it rising to the second-floor screening with a cathedral-like effect.

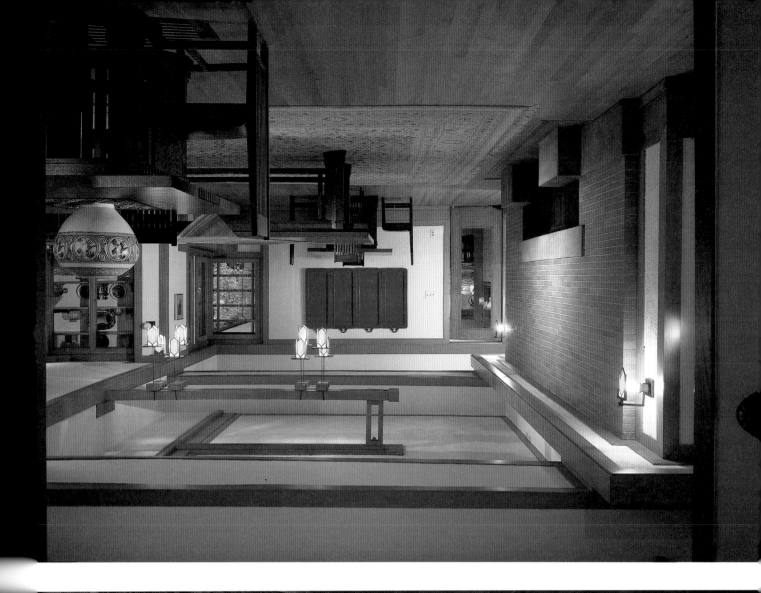

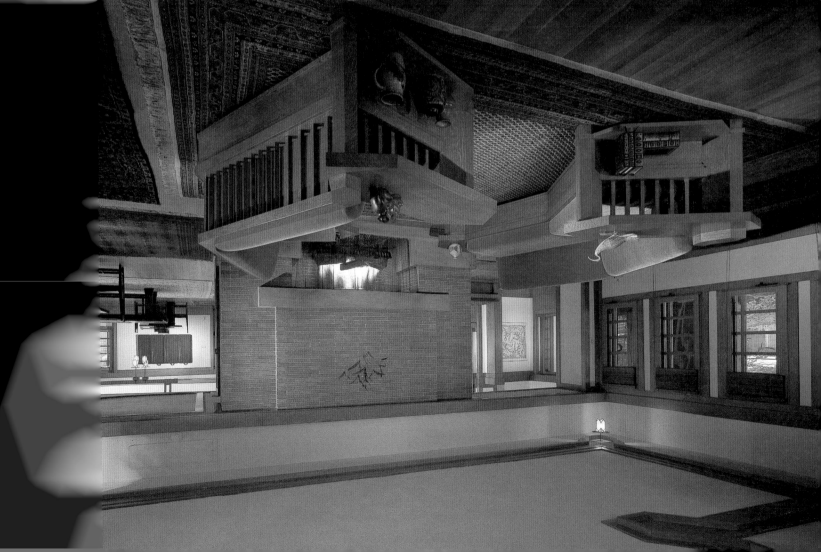

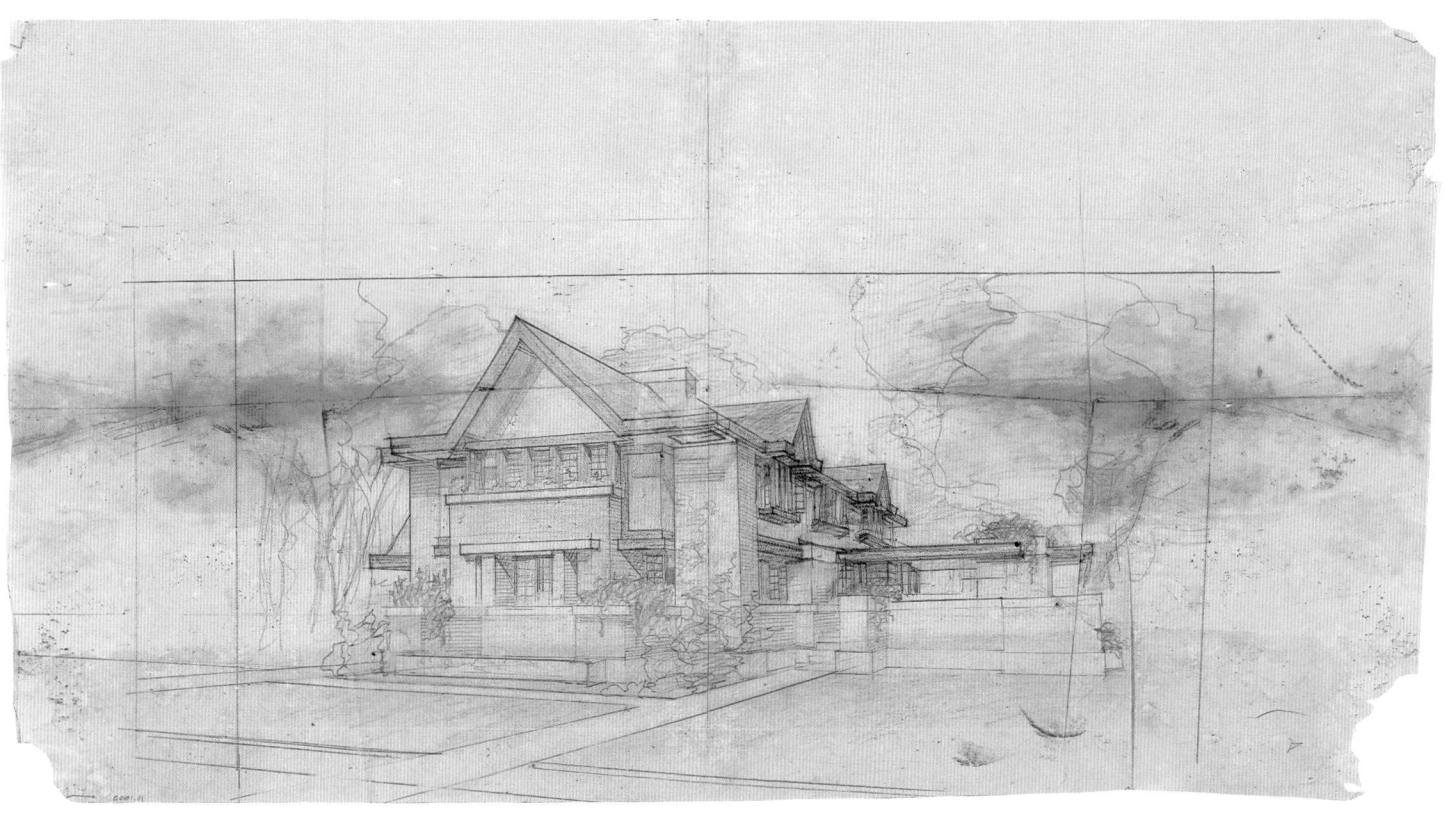

Opposite top: The open floor plan of the Beachy house allows generous space for the living room, with its great fireplace of hand-formed Roman brick. Oak forms the window frames, stringcourses, and flooring. The wide plaster band below the high ceiling humanizes the scale.

Opposite bottom: The long rectangular dining room has its own capacious hearth and the original cherry-wood furniture and lighting fixtures designed by Wright. A built-in china closet occupies an alcove.

Above: Perspective of the Beachy house, which has a horizontal plan, with projecting porches that make it look even larger than it is. *The Frank Lloyd Wright Archives, © The Frank Lloyd Wright Foundation.*

Right: A chair made for the Beachy house to Wright's specifications in 1906 and now in the collection of the Virginia Museum of Fine Arts. Dining Room Chair, 1906. Oak, upholstery, 46″ H × 14⅜″ W × 18″ D. *Gift of Sydney and Frances Lewis, Virginia Museum of Fine Arts, Richmond, VA (85.78).*

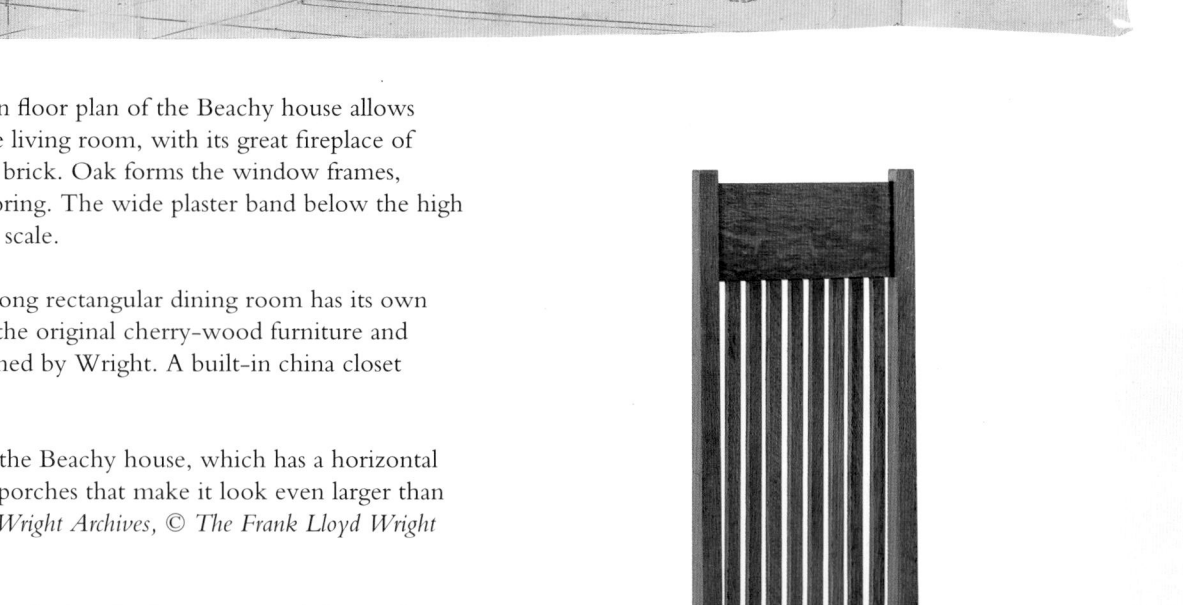

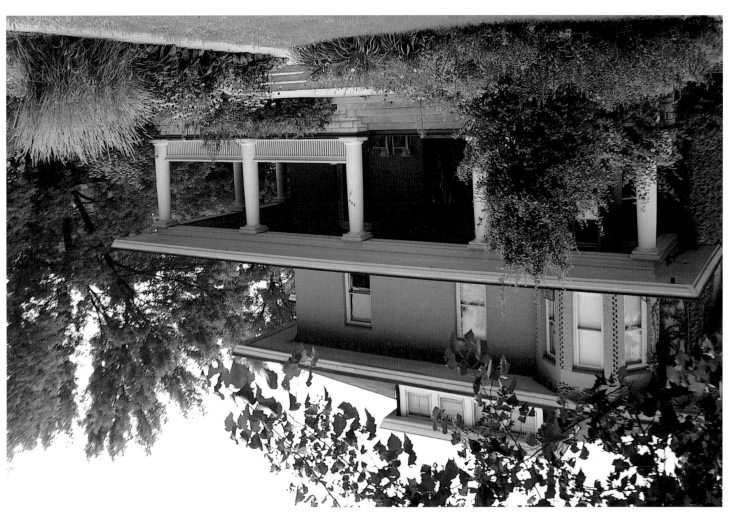

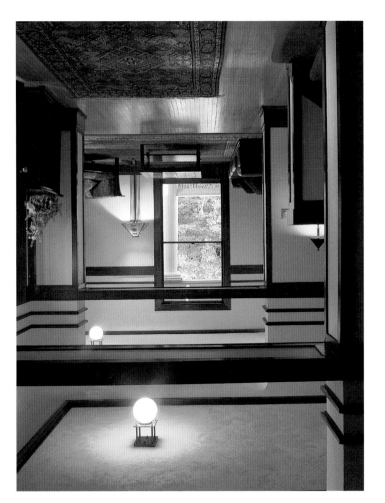

William H. Copeland House,
1909

400 North Forest Avenue

Right: The Copeland house was another extensive remodeling, in which Wright replaced architraves with horizontal stringcourses to scale down the original eleven-foot ceiling.

Below: The second floor of the Copeland house remains largely as built. On the first floor, many of Wright's plans for the exterior were not carried out. The roofline and dormer, porch, and entryway were altered to his design.

Opposite: The original boxlike rooms of the Copeland residence were opened up to permit free-flowing spaces on the ground floor. The dining room furniture and doors were designed by Wright, and the stairwell was remodeled.

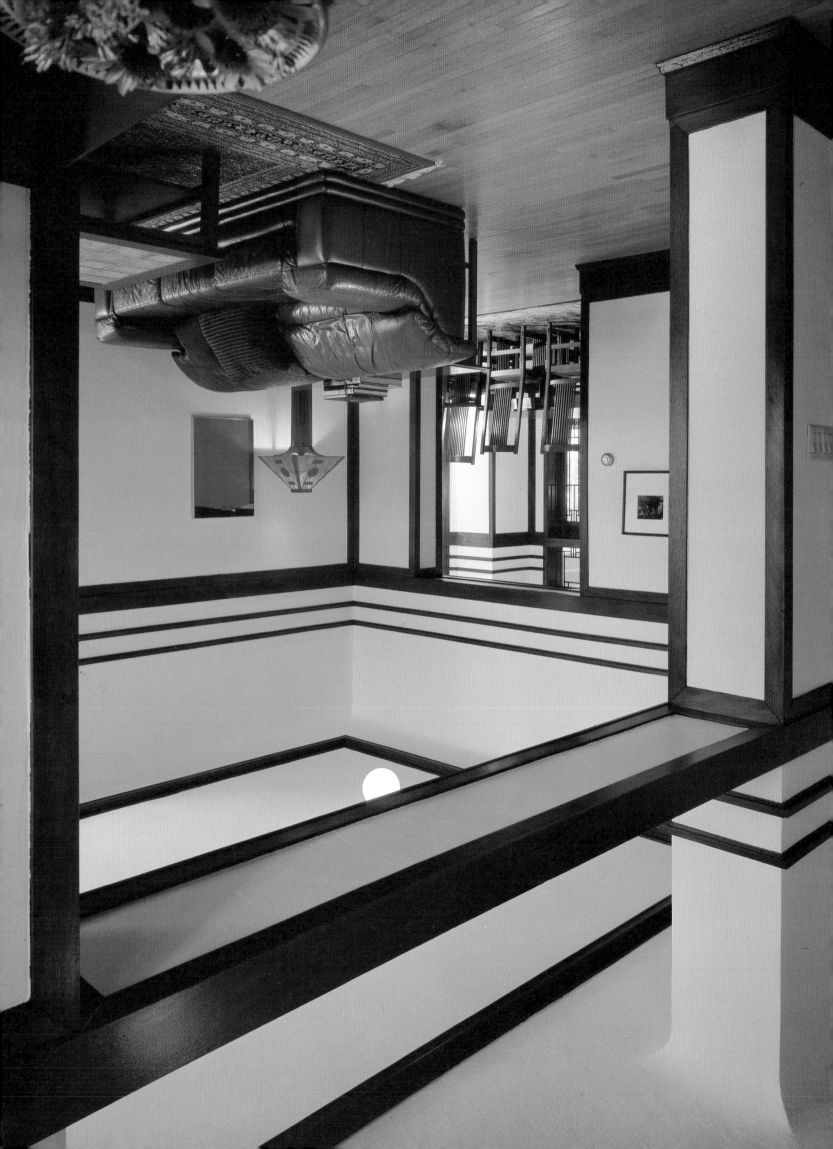

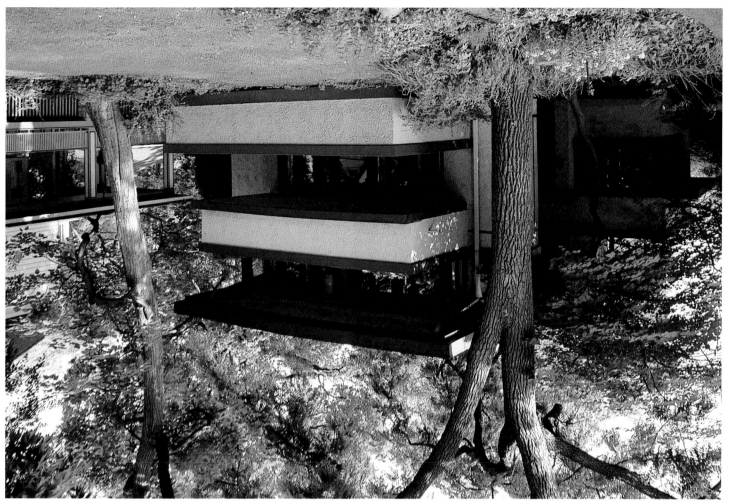

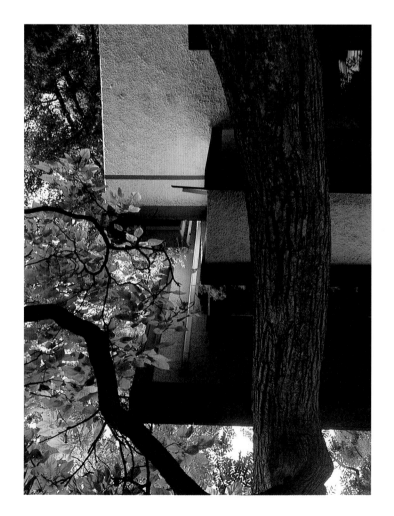

Mrs. Thomas (Laura) Gale House, 1909

6 Elizabeth Court

Below: After she was widowed, Mrs. Thomas Gale asked Wright to design a second home for her. Roughly square in plan, it is plaster-surfaced and trimmed in wood. The use of cantilever design principles led Wright and others to link it to Fallingwater, but according to Storrer, its prototype was the unbuilt, flat-roofed Yahara Boat Club project of 1902.

Right: Exterior detail showing the cantilevered balcony of the second-floor bedroom with its corner windows.

Opposite: Replica dining room of the Laura Gale house, with clear-glass windows on three sides and furniture and fixtures designed by Wright.

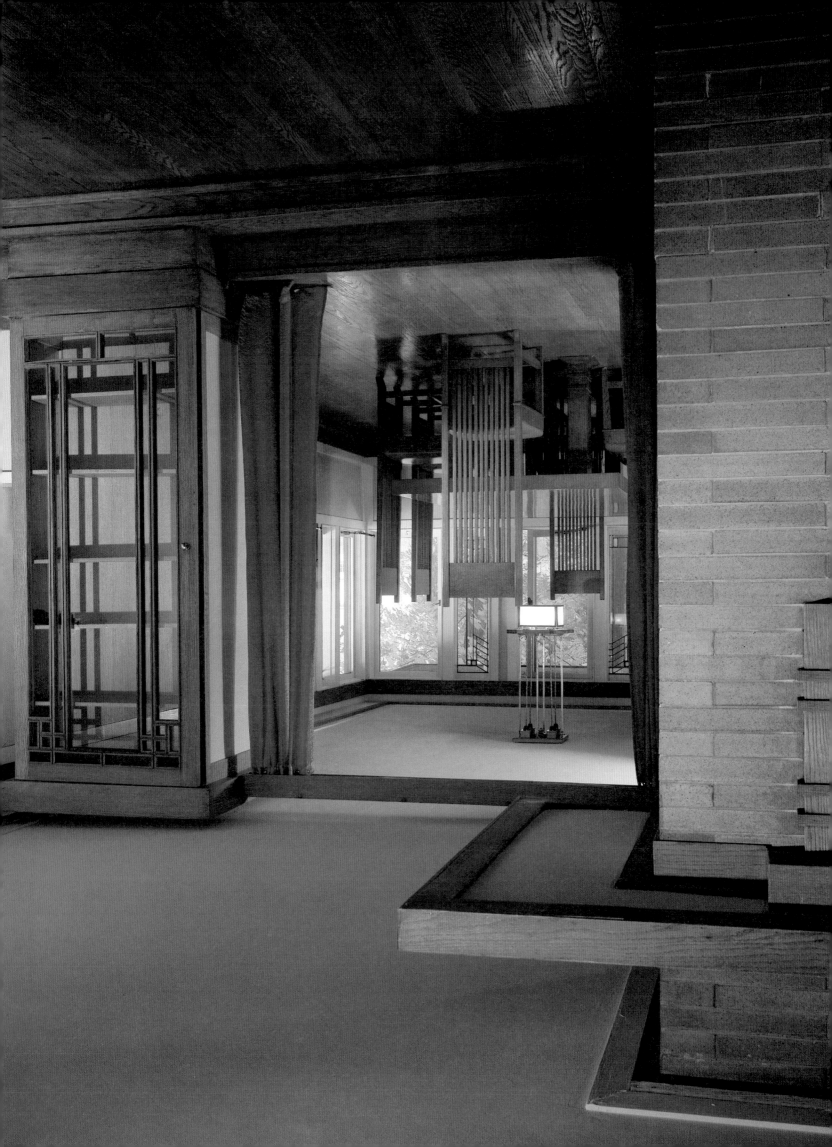

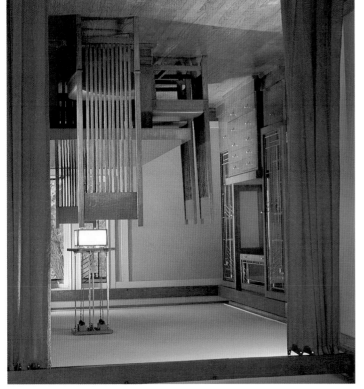

Above: Perspective of the Prairie house designed for Mrs. Thomas Gale in 1904 but not constructed until 1909. Thus it predated the landmark Robie house in Chicago and was contemporaneous with Unity Temple. *The Frank Lloyd Wright Archives, © The Frank Lloyd Wright Foundation.*

Right: Dining room of the Gale house, with built-in oak sideboard and shelving. It is set off from the living room by a two-step rise.

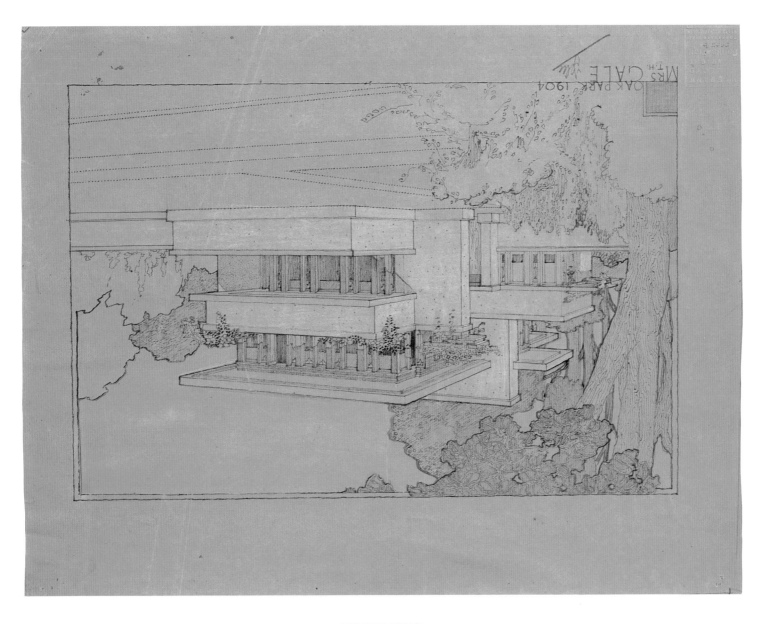

Oscar B. Balch House, 1911

611 North Kenilworth Avenue

Below: This two-story Prairie house was designed for decorator Oscar Balch after Wright's extended stay in Europe. It is on a symmetrical axis atypical of Wright's work at this period. The living room overlooks the terrace. The house has fifty windows, most of them of the casement type.

Right: The main entrance to the Balch house is entirely concealed, and a security wall almost surrounds the residence. The color pattern has been changed from the original white plaster with dark wood trim, to good effect.

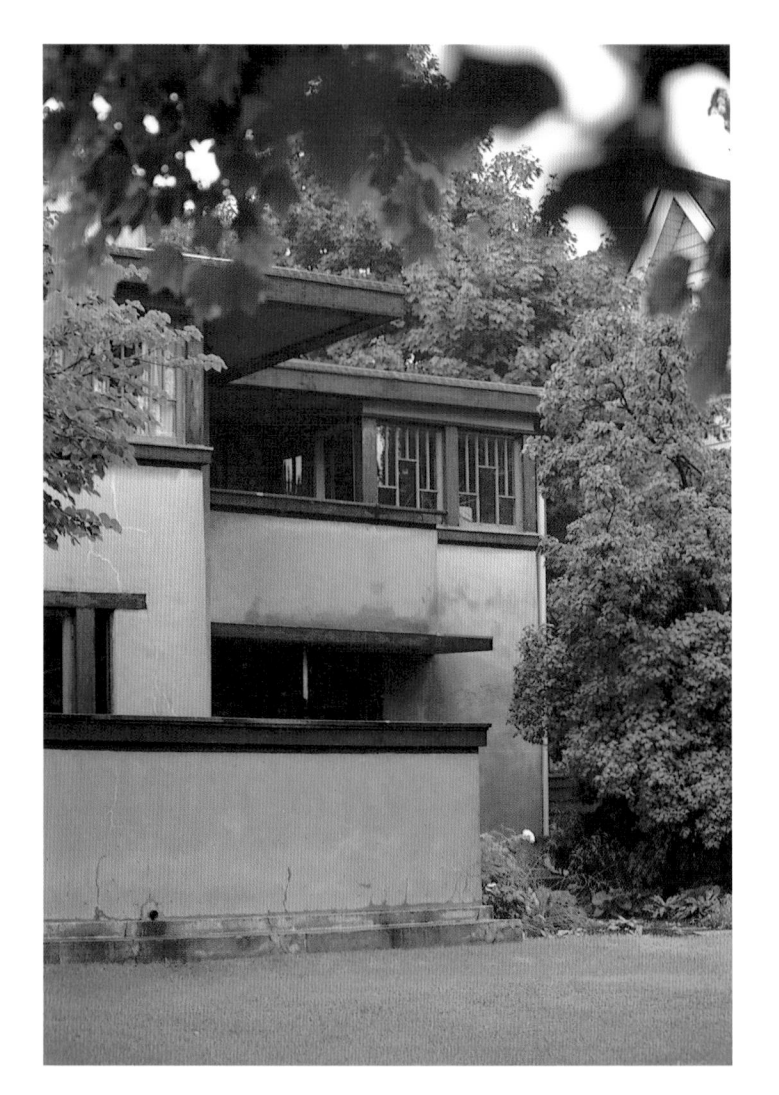

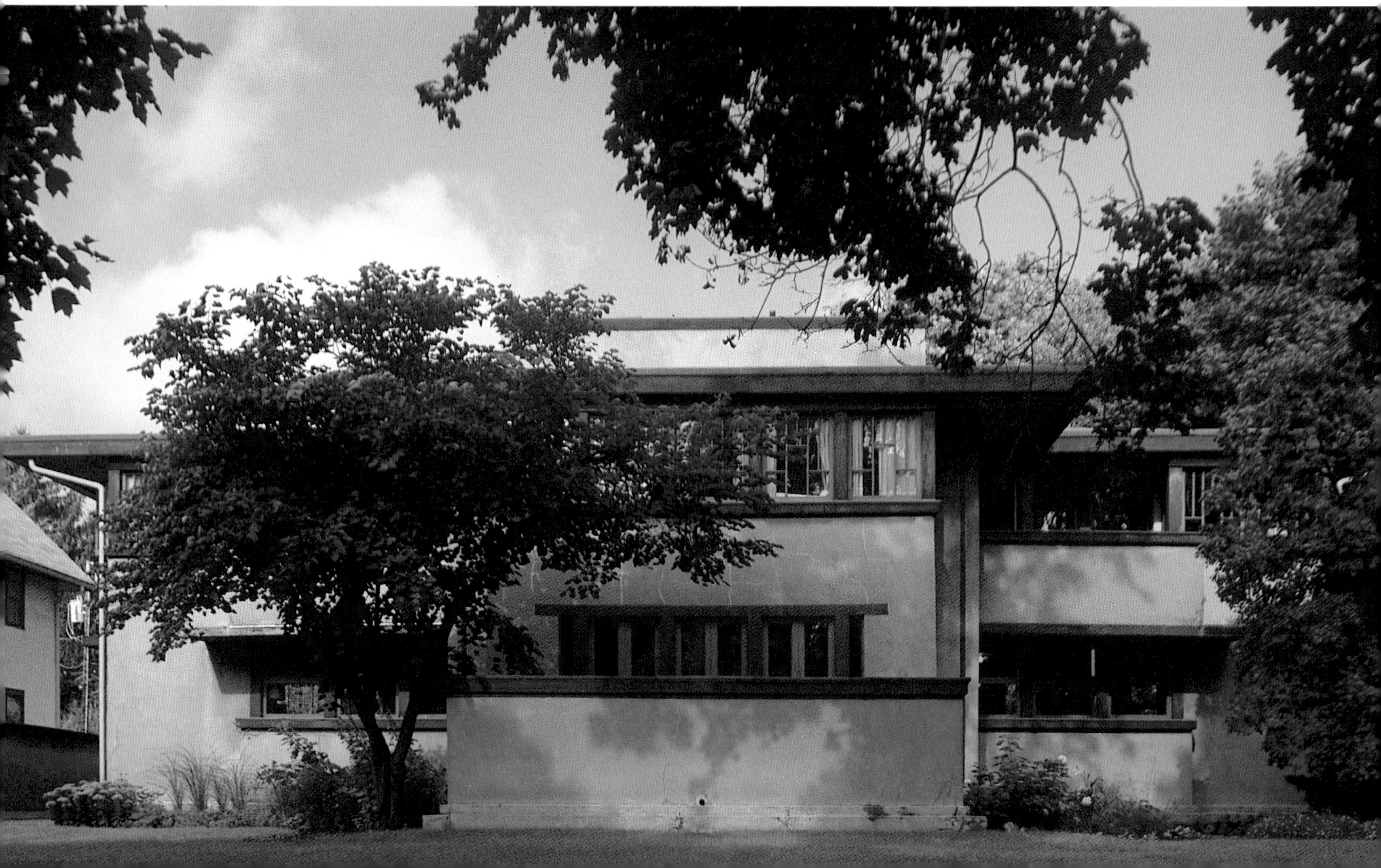

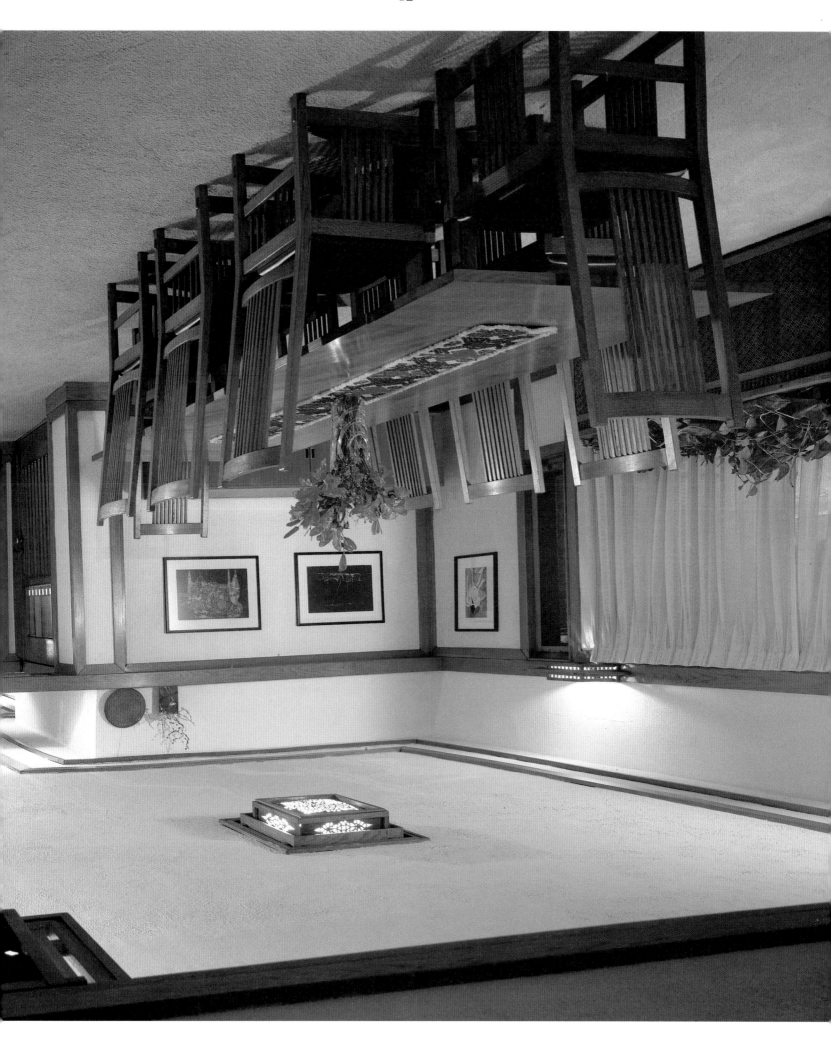

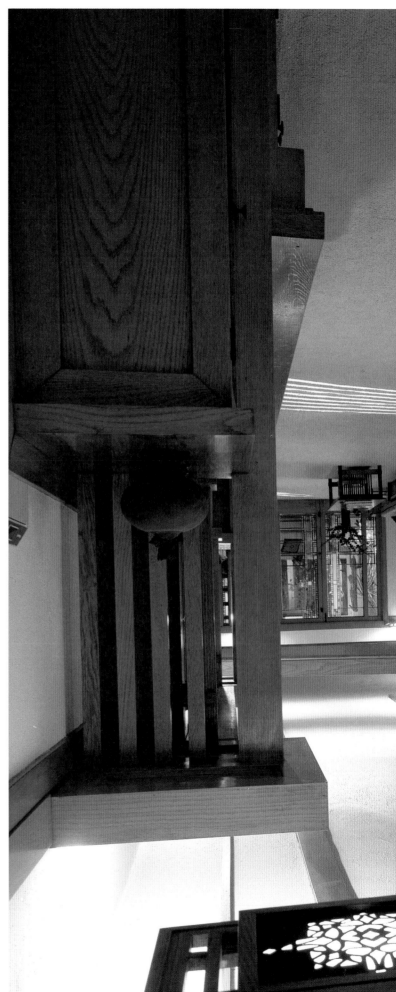

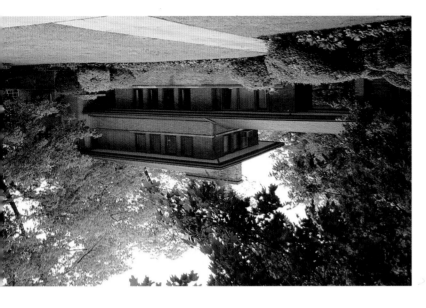

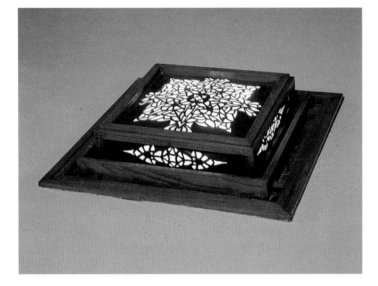

Harry S. Adams House, 1913
710 West Augusta Street

Left: The vista from the dining room through the hall of the Harry S. Adams house is seventy feet long. Wright's interior includes furniture, moldings, fixtures, and window glass of his design. In 1940, modern architect Mies van der Rohe would recall how he and other young modernists in Europe had been inspired by the "clarity of language and the disconcerting richness of form" in Wright's work.

Below: Recessed lighting and copper ceiling grids contribute to the ambience of the Adams house.

Bottom: The two-story brick Adams house, Wright's last work in Oak Park, has limestone banding at both sill levels and a porte cochere that extends the horizontal line of the structure. It is a summation of the Prairie house ideal at the time when Wright was returning to new interests and objectives.

Oak Park Visitors Information

Oak Park Visitors Center
158 North Forest Avenue
Oak Park, IL 60301
708-848-1500

Frank Lloyd Wright Home and Studio
951 Chicago Avenue
Oak Park, IL 60302
708-848-1976
Owned by the National Trust for Historic Preservation and managed by the Frank Lloyd Wright Home and Studio Foundation

Frank Lloyd Wright Prairie School of Architecture, National Historic District
Ginkgo Tree Bookshop
951 Chicago Avenue
Oak Park, IL 60302
708-848-1976
Audio and map guided tours

Unity Temple
875 West Lake Street
Oak Park, IL 60302
708-383-8873
National Historic Landmark

Historical Society of Oak Park and River Forest
217 Home Avenue
Oak Park, IL 60303
708-848-6755

The publisher and photographers wish to thank the many homeowners who generously opened their homes for this project.

Below: Detail of the second floor entry from the exterior deck of the Frank W. Thomas house.

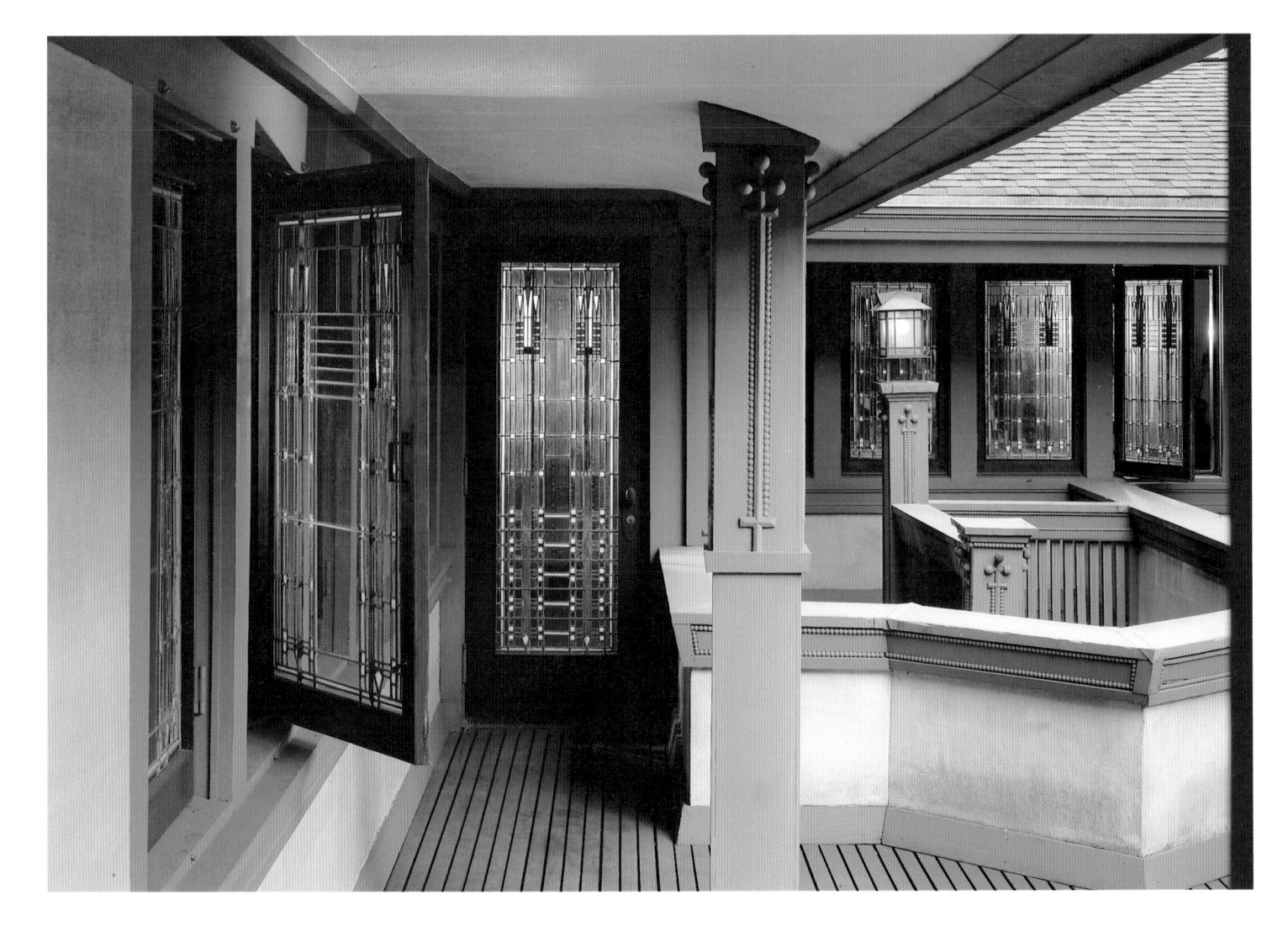